RICHARD AND PHILIP: THE BURTONS

Philip Burton

RICHARD & PHILIP
THE BURTONS

A Book of Memories

With a Foreword by
ELIZABETH TAYLOR

Peter Owen · London

To Kate with love

PETER OWEN PUBLISHERS
73 Kenway Road London SW5 0RE

First published in Great Britain 1992
© Philip Burton 1992

The extract on page 13 from *A Christmas Story* by Richard Burton, published by Hodder and Stoughton, appears by kind permission of Mrs Sally Burton.

The endpapers are based on a photograph of Richard and Philip Burton with Elizabeth Taylor at a poetry reading in New York, 1964. (Photograph: Friedman-Abeles)

All Rights Reserved.
No part of this publication may be reproduced in any form or by any means without the written permission of the publishers.

A catalogue record for this book is available from the British Library

ISBN 0-7206-0855-4

Printed in Great Britain by Billings of Worcester

Preface

This is not a biography of Richard Burton. It is a collection of memories of an association that lasted over forty years. I shall not attempt even to sketch his career, but shall deal only with those parts of it with which I had some personal connection. And I shall say something about my own life and career too.

I had been urged by several people to tell the story of how the Welsh teenager Richard Jenkins became the actor of world renown Richard Burton, but I hesitated to do so because I feared the result would sound as if I were blowing my own trumpet. I have now been made to realize that I should tell the story because of its inherent interest and because it will reveal a Richard that those who have written about him did not know. I owe it to Richard and to those who loved and admired him.

My memory has been helped by small diaries I have kept since 1950, five years to a page, and by some of the material from my book *Early Doors*.

Foreword

Without Philip Burton there never would have been a Richard Burton. That great rolling voice that cracked like wild Atlantic waves would never have been heard outside the valley. Those green cat-eyes would have broken probably only a few hundred hearts instead of millions. The myriad of songs in his brain would never have found their outlet in poetry. His vast love and profound knowledge of poetry would never have been heard because they never would have been channeled.

A teacher named Philip Burton saw in a wild young man called Richie Jenkins that 'divine spark of fire' that could open the kingdom of knowledge to him for the rest of his life and change him forever.

This story is Philip's, the story of an adoptive father's great love and devotion, and of a great teacher and how he helped one of the most fascinating, brilliant and magnificent men of any age.

I for one thank you, Phil, because if it hadn't been for you I probably would never have met Richard – I thank you with all my life for that.

Elizabeth Taylor

CHAPTER
One

One day in 1964, while Richard was playing in *Hamlet* on Broadway, he and I were interviewed jointly in a private corner of an Eighth Avenue bar and restaurant much frequented by theatre people. We had a live audience of one, Richard's wife Elizabeth Taylor. One of the questions aimed at me was, 'How did you come to adopt him?' For reasons that will become apparent I hesitated in order to make a true and careful answer, and Richard jumped in with 'He didn't adopt me; I adopted him.' There was much truth in that. He needed me and, as I realized later, he set out to get me.

I have no recollection of our first meeting, but he often reminded me of it, jokingly, because I turned him down for a paid acting job. It must have been in 1937 or '38, when he was twelve or thirteen. I was the Senior Master at the Port Talbot Secondary School in South Wales. My teaching was confined to the senior pupils, and he was a junior. At that time I was already writing for the British Broadcasting Corporation's radio station in Cardiff, some thirty miles away, and I had just written a play about the boyhood of William Shakespeare. I needed three or four boys in the cast, and the director had suggested that I should get them from my school so that I could coach them, and in particular give them a satisfactory English accent. Apparently Richard eagerly presented himself for an audition and interview, but his Welsh accent was so strong – he spoke Welsh at home – that I dismissed him immediately.

Had it not been for World War II, Richard and I would

probably never have met again. In 1939 the Guild of Graduates of the University of Wales announced an award of a scholarship of a sabbatical year to some graduate already well established in a profession. I'm sure many hundreds applied. Ultimately the award was shared by two men, each to have a six-month sabbatical: the Professor of Agriculture at the University College of Aberystwyth, and me. Both of us decided to spend the time in the USA, but we never met. I explored some of the high schools of New York City, and was more impressed by their problems than their achievements, until I chanced upon the Horace Mann School for Boys, and Alfred Baruth, the Head of the English Department and a notable teacher. He took me to his home and introduced me to his wife, Charlotte, and his two daughters. (Some years later Richard was to meet them when he was undergoing training in Canada for the Royal Air Force.) The Baruths became my good friends. (Alas, both are now dead.) They had previously conducted summer tours of Europe for the senior pupils in the school, but as the Hitler menace grew, especially after the Munich settlement in 1937, they changed to America, and I was richly blessed in joining the 1939 tour. We went in large cars all the way to Mexico City, and then one half of the party explored the Pacific coast of the USA, while Charlotte took the other half to Hawaii. War became imminent as we recrossed the country, and we arrived in New York City on the evening of Wednesday 30 August. War was declared on Sunday 3 September.

I was strongly urged and received several inducements to stay in New York, but I was determined to get home as soon as I could. I had a return booking on the *Aquitania*, but she was held in port by the American authorities, as were the ships of other countries combatant in Europe.

The *President Roosevelt* was going to venture the transatlantic crossing, and I managed to get a booking on her. She set sail on 6 September, with the Stars and Stripes painted prominently on her sides and floodlit at night. We had been warned that our most likely destination would be in Portugal, but we did in fact land at Southampton on 15 September.

While I was in America I had virtually made up my mind to leave schoolteaching and devote my life to writing and acting for the theatre and the BBC, but the war changed all that. The Ministry of Labour decided that I had to resume my position in the Port Talbot Secondary School. For the six years of the war I was not only a very busy schoolmaster, but did a lot of work for BBC Radio in Cardiff, and became the leader, with the rank of Flight Lieutenant, of Squadron 499 of the Air Training Corps. The aim of the ATC was to give as much prior training as possible to future members of the RAF; membership was, of course, voluntary.

Richard was to benefit greatly from all three of my wartime activities: from my teaching in the school and in private; from my radio work as a result of which he first became a professional actor; and from his becoming an ATC cadet, which opened the way to his going to Oxford University for six months before joining the RAF. But much was to happen before he became an integral part of my life.

Years later he found a diary he had kept as a schoolboy in 1940, two years before I became really aware of him, and he gave it to me. There are thirteen references to me in it, all of them complimentary; sometimes I appear as 'Burton' and at other times as 'Mr Burton'. The first, on Shrove Tuesday, 6 February, reads: 'Had a fine afternoon especially with Burton who talked about Astronomy.' I cannot imagine how I came to talk about that subject, of which I have no special knowledge. His overriding interest in the diary is rugby football, and he never lost that interest. For purposes of competition the pupils in the school were divided into houses. One house was called Leisan, and I was the Head; it chanced that Richard also belonged to it. The entry for 6 November, four days before his fifteenth birthday, reads: 'Leisan House had a meeting. I was picked captain of football in Leisan. Cliff Owen and I both had equal votes and the chairman Mr Burton came my way.' As I reflect on that, it seems to me remarkable that a barely fifteen-year-old boy should be chosen captain of a team which almost certainly contained boys two years older than he.

Nearly every Sunday starts with the entry, 'Chapel all day.' Nonconformist places of worship in Wales were all called chapels. 'Church' was restricted to Church of England and Roman Catholic places of worship, and though the former had become disestablished by Act of Parliament, it was, and is, known as the Church in Wales. Welsh was the language of the chapel Richard attended, and he and many others found a weekly joy in the singing. Even after he came to live with me, he still joined the family at chapel every Sunday.

There are frequent references in his diary to air raids, sometimes two or three in the same day. Port Talbot had a large and vital steelworks, and moonlit nights almost always brought the Luftwaffe, but they also came in daylight. The diary records no fear of the bombings. I remember that, a few years later, when I took Richard to London for the first time, we experienced a very heavy raid. I thought he was following me and other hotel guests to the shelter, but he wasn't; he had gone up to the roof 'to watch it all'. The diary records that even when the family went to a nearby shelter he would stay in bed.

Mention of the family prompts me to say something about Richard's background. Pontrhydyfen, a village in the valley a few miles north of Port Talbot, is almost invariably described as his Welsh home town. It's true that he was born there, but he was taken from there at the age of two and brought up in Taibach, the eastern part of Port Talbot. Richard was the twelfth of thirteen children, two of whom died in infancy. There were seven boys and six girls. His mother died at forty-four, soon after giving birth to the last boy, Graham. The eldest brother, Thomas Henry, took care of Graham, and the eldest sister, Cecilia ('Cis'), took care of Richard. Cis had married a coal miner, Elfed James, by whom she had two daughters.

Richard could not have loved a mother more than he loved the beautiful and admirable Cecilia, who fully returned the love of the growing boy; he was to her the son she never had. Here is Richard's tribute to her in his delightful little book *A Christmas Story*, which was published in 1964:

Now my sister was no ordinary woman – no woman ever is, but to me, my sister less than any. When my mother had died, she, my sister, had become my mother, and more mother to me than any mother could ever have been. I was immensely proud of her. I shone in the reflection of her green-eyed, black-haired, gypsy beauty. She sang at her work in a voice so pure that the local men said she had a bell in every tooth, and was gifted by God. And these pundits who revelled in music of any kind and had agreed many times, with much self-congratulations, that of all instruments devised by man, crwth, violin, pibcorn, dulcimer, viola, church organ, zither, harp, brass band, woodwind, or symphony orchestra – they had smugly agreed that there was no noise as beautiful at its best as the sound of the human voice.

She had a throat that should have been coloured with down like a small bird, and eyes so hazel-green and open that, to preserve them from too much knowledge of evil, should have been hooded and vultured and not, as they were, terrible in their vulnerability. She was innocent and guileless and infinitely protectable. She was naive to the point of saintliness, and wept a lot at the misery of others. She felt all tragedies except her own. I had read of the Knights of Chivalry and I knew that I had a bounden duty to protect her above all other creatures.

Things were difficult for Elfed, and I can understand and sympathize with his position and his attitude to Richard. A coal miner's life was never easy, and the years when Richard was growing up were particularly difficult years of depression, strikes, lay-offs, part-time work; every penny counted. In his diary Richard carefully recorded every one of those pennies he was given or earned, the latter chiefly by collecting newspapers to be used as wrappers in fish and chip shops. To Elfed, Richard was a potential wage-earner, and there he was in school, costing money, not earning it. And the situation was made more bitter for Elfed by the fact that neither of his daughters, Marian and Rhianon, had won a place in the secondary school, to which entrance was gained by a competitive examination. I feel sure that his wife's deep and protective love for the boy also irked Elfed.

There are several references in the diary to rows with Elfed. Sometimes the causes were trifling, as when Richard returned some books to the library including one that Elfed had wanted to read. Incidentally, the diary records many borrowings of library books but not once is a title mentioned. On two occasions the quarrels with Elfed caused Richard to leave home, hoping to find a place with some other member of the family, but it didn't work out, and the second time, be it to Elfed's credit, it was he who asked the boy to return, presumably at the urging of Cis.

There's a very revealing entry for Tuesday 21 May. Elfed must have got hold of the diary. I don't know how much of it he read, but the entry for 20 May seems to have galled him because it told him that the potential wage-earner had spent much of the day playing cricket. He wrote in the diary, 'At four o'clock Richard Walter shits his pants.' Since this was written in pencil, why didn't Richard erase it? It seems he wanted to preserve the evidence of Elfed's attitude to him. He even added a comment: 'This was written by Elfed in an attempt to spoil the Book, but it will remain if I live to be 100.'

A poignant reflection on the situation occurs in the entries for Thursday 10 and Friday 11 October. Thursday: 'Had a terrible row today; Elfed told me to go back to Pontrhydyfen. I walked as far as Cwmavon. I hate the sight of Elfed. I am going to ask Daddy to take me back home where I can go to work. I could never stay home now.' Friday: 'I intended to go to Ponty but I have cooled off a bit now. Cis wants me to go if I want to. But I am sure that wherever I go I will not be wanted, the same as here.'

One entry in the diary completely surprised me because I never knew him to evince any pride in possessions. On Wednesday 25 August he writes: 'I have been flaunting different ties every day. I have about 40 ties, all different.'

In the light of his future, the most significant entries have to do with his first part in the annual school play. The week's run of the play had become quite an institution in the cultural life of the town. I always chose worthwhile plays, notably those of Shakespeare and Shaw. That year's play was Shaw's *The Apple Cart*, and Richard received the part of Mr Vanhattan, the American Ambassador in London. Richard regretted that he appeared only in the second act. His entry for Thursday 19 September reads: 'Supposed to play football but went to Burton instead. Had a nice time. He told me to modulate my voice a little more as I sounded like a gangster not an American who had been educated.' I have to confess that I have no recollection of his performance.

The situation at home reached a climax in the early months of 1941, and Richard had to leave school. He began work in the clothing department of the Co-operative store in Taibach. That would have been the end of this story had it not been for Meredith Jones. He had been one of Richard's teachers in the Taibach Elementary School; he had also run a youth club in connection with the school, and Richard had been a very active member of it. Meredith was impressed by Richard's potential, though he didn't know in what field it would express itself. He was dismayed to find that the boy had been robbed of his educational opportunity, and he set about to right the wrong, which wasn't easy; places in the school were too precious to be treated so lightly. I know that he canvassed the governors of the school, but first he must have persuaded Elfed to change his mind, in itself a hard task, I feel sure. It took eighteen months to get Richard reinstated, and once the return was certain Meredith came to see me. We were both involved in the ATC, he being one of my officers. He was concerned about the changes that might have occurred in Richard as a result of his year and a half 'out in the world'. He feared that the boy might have become a little wild and therefore have a bad influence in the school. I was the master Richard most respected; would I keep an eye on him?

Richard returned to school a month before his seventeenth birthday. As a result of his lost schooling he couldn't rejoin his previous class, and so was at least a year older than the other boys and girls in the class to which he was assigned. With his experience of the world he was now a young man among kids.

He took two steps which brought him into contact with me: he joined the ATC squadron, and he saw to it that he did fire-watch duty on my nights. Every night some of the older boys, under the charge of a master, had to maintain watch at the school because of the air raids. In particular they had to deal with any firebombs that might get lodged on the roof. Richard's fire watching finally resulted in his coming to live with me.

I lived as a sort of paying guest – the word 'lodger' was anathema to the family – with a Mrs Smith and her two daughters. 'Ma Smith', as we called her in genuine appreciation of her care for us, was a remarkable lady. She was the widow of a maritime chief engineer, with whom she had done much travelling. In 1917 he had come home on leave and had fallen victim to the widespread and lethal flu epidemic of that year; because he had died ashore and off-duty, his widow was paid little compensation. Suddenly she found herself faced with having to make a living for herself and two children. Lacking any particular skill or training, she decided to take in paying guests. I became one in 1925, the year Richard was born, and I happily stayed with her when she subsequently moved twice. The house in which we lived in 1942 was fairly large; it had four bedrooms and a bathroom upstairs, and three living rooms and a kitchen downstairs. Mrs Smith and her daughters shared the commodious front bedroom, mine was next to it, and beyond the bathroom were two small bedrooms, the first occupied by an engineer in the steelworks, and the second by a bank clerk. Downstairs the large front room was mine, and the middle room was the engineer's; the bank clerk had no separate living room.

During our fire watching Richard seized every opportunity for private talks with me, which were often interrupted by air-raid warnings. I soon became very interested by his undoubted potential – but for what? He was developing an acute social and political conscience, and I could see him devoting his life to the Labour Party and becoming a second Aneurin Bevan, who had begun his career by working in a coal mine at the age of thirteen and had risen to be the Labour Party's most brilliant orator and a cabinet minister in three governments. When Richard had applied for re-admission to the school he had had to state his professional ambition. He had said, probably on the advice of Meredith Jones, that it was schoolteaching. When he told me that he wanted to be an actor like Owen Jones, I was very surprised but instinctively excited and challenged. Owen Jones was a former protégé of mine who came from a Welsh-speaking home and, under my tutelage, had won a valuable and much sought-after open scholarship, the Leverhulme, to the Royal Academy of Dramatic Art in London. During the war he became an officer in the RAF, and he died while in the service, thus cutting off a very promising career. In 1937 he had played Laertes to Olivier's Hamlet at the Old Vic. (In 1978 Richard gave me a copy of A.L. Rowse's three-volume illustrated edition of Shakespeare. I immediately turned to *Hamlet* in volume III, confidently expecting to see a picture of Richard in the title role. Instead, the book contained a picture of a scene between Olivier and Owen Jones.) I told Richard that, if he wanted to become a professional actor, he first had to change both the quality of his voice and his speech, and that would involve hard and tiresome work. His response was, 'All right – change 'em.'

He began to tell me the difficulties of his life at home, and finally he told me that he had tried more than once to move in with another brother or sister, but they had persuaded him to return to Cis and Elfed. I am sure that they had a twofold motivation: reluctance to be burdened with a teenager who wasn't earning a wage, and the consideration of how much he meant to Cis. One night I was so touched by yet another account of his plight that I mentioned, without realizing the full implication of what I was saying, that there was a spare bedroom in Mrs Smith's house. (The bank clerk had been called up by the army.) He seized on it and asked when he could move in. I immediately backtracked, and he said with a sorrow that made me feel guilty, 'When push comes to shove, nobody wants me.' I began to defend my withdrawal. I told him that soon he would be in the air force and no longer a financial burden on Elfed.

More than that, when the war was over he would be a wage-earner at something or other, and would be able to help Elfed and Cis. Elfed was already well aware, I said, that the liability he resented would one day become an asset he would welcome. I felt sure that he, and still more Cis, would now be unwilling for Richard to leave. His reply was, 'Ask Elfed, that's all, ask 'im.' I had to agree to do so, and it was arranged that I would go to Taibach the following Sunday afternoon. In the meantime I discussed with Mrs Smith the slight possibility of Richard's coming to live in her house, taking the empty bedroom and sharing the living room with me. She would, of course, be happy to have the lost income restored, but she had also met Richard and liked him; he, and other pupils, had occasionally come to the house in connection with some school activity.

I have vivid memories of that Sunday-afternoon meeting with Elfed and Cis in the front room of 73 Caradog Street. I had gone there determined to use every argument I could muster to keep Richard living with the James family. I had not met Cis or Elfed before.

Richard was not in the room. My first impression was of the Madonna-like beauty of Cis. She sat silent while the vigorous Elfed did all the talking with me. His answer to everything I said was, 'You take 'im, Mr Burton, you take 'im.' I promised that his further education would be no burden to them, and that, after the war, I would see to it that he received a free college education, which should not be denied him, but all I got was, 'You take 'im, Mr Burton, you take 'im.' Finally, in order to have a word with the silent Cis, I asked Elfed to fetch Richard, who had been awaiting in the kitchen the result of the meeting. Reluctantly Elfed left the room and I said to Cis, 'Richie is your son much more than your brother, and I know how much you love each other. What do you want me to do?' Her reply, which changed not only Richard's life but mine too, was, 'If you take him it would be the answer to my prayers.' When Elfed returned with Richard, I told them I would do as they all wished, and the room seemed to be filled with the happiness of relief.

CHAPTER
Two

It was 1 March 1943 when Richard moved into 6 Connaught Street, Port Talbot. As he often pointed out, it was a most appropriate date because it was St David's Day, the national day of Wales in honour of its patron saint. In later years Richard sometimes remembered to send me a cable on 1 March in commemoration of 'our day'.

He was always fiercely proud of being Welsh. He called his home in Switzerland Le Pays de Galles, French for Wales. This pride was particularly apparent when the Welsh rugby team engaged in international competition; everyone would wait with bated breath until the result was known. When Richard married Sybil Williams in February 1949, the wedding party was held in the London home of Daphne Rye, who was an important member of the staff of H.M. Tennent, the biggest and best theatre producer in London (the company was owned and run by Hugh Beaumont). Daphne had been the first London professional to sense Richard's potential when she weeded out actors in Cardiff for parts in *The Druid's Rest*. I was present at the wedding party, in the middle of which Sybil, the new bride, had to leave for a matinée of *Harvey*; she had a small part and was also an assistant stage manager and understudy. Richard also disappeared. He had gone upstairs to listen to a radio broadcast of an international rugby match between Wales and Scotland. The result soured his day; Wales lost.

Richard rarely gloated over a performance, but his Welsh pride came to the fore in a letter he wrote to me in November

19

1958. It came from Switzerland and was sent to New York City, where I had been living for more than four years. Under my guidance and influence he had first established himself as a radio actor in the Welsh Service of the BBC, but he had long left it for the London theatre and Hollywood films; yet in 1958 he made a special return. 'I finally did something I haven't done for years,' he writes. 'I broadcast for the Welsh region, and, something I've never done, I did a play in Welsh. It was a new play of Saunders-Lewis, *Brad*, meaning Treason. I thoroughly enjoyed doing it.' Then he mentions four prominent London actors who had also originally come from Wales and had returned to take part in the important production. 'I didn't have as much difficulty with the Welsh as the others, I thought. I also recorded the death speech of Llewellyn Olaf, quite a long speech, for Aneirin, to be part of the Albert Hall do on St David's Day. That too seemed alright.' The late Aneirin Talfan Davies was a fine Welsh scholar and a good friend of mine.

I have no Welsh blood – both my parents were born in England – but Welsh was a compulsory subject in the high school at which I was a pupil, and I became so adept in it as a written language that I even won a prize for it. But that literary Welsh was very different from the colloquial language, and so Richard and I never attempted a Welsh conversation. However, when we lived together he often sought my help on questions of Welsh grammar. In his 1940 diary it was clear that he had been much more concerned about his marks in Welsh than those in any other subject.

During the war years I was kept very busy with my school work, the BBC and the ATC, but whenever there was a spare hour I devoted it to the training of Richard, chiefly in our living room in 6 Connaught Street. It meant a lot of hard work for both of us, but he was an admirable student. First we had to work on his voice and his speech. I aimed at giving him what I call mid-Atlantic speech, which is equally acceptable in London and New York. The vowel sounds must be clearly distinguished and the consonantal sounds distinct. The so-called Oxford accent of the English elite does not distinguish between 'man' and 'men', and many educated Americans do not distinguish sufficiently between 'sale' and 'sell'. As for words with successive consonantal sounds... ! I readily admit that English is a difficult language, but many an American who is paid a handsome salary to speak on radio or television doesn't take the trouble to pronounce properly a word like 'asked'; most of them make it 'ast'. If professional speakers don't accept the discipline of accuracy and clarity, what hope is there for our language? Richard readily accepted that discipline.

As for the quality of his voice, it was adolescent rough to begin with, but with constant practice it became memorably beautiful. In order to teach him not to shout for emphasis, we used to go up the mountain that overlooked Port Talbot for a special exercise. We would separate and the distance between us was decided by his continued ability to hear my ordinary speech. Then he would recite something, a speech by the Chorus from *Henry V* for example, and he soon learned that it was distinctness, not volume, that mattered.

Never did I let up on his speech, sometimes to our mutual embarrassment. We would be having a serious, intimate talk, and I would break in with, 'Stop! Say that again.'

I soon discovered that he had a natural feeling for poetry, essential poetry. By that I do not mean that which often passes for poetry these days, but is really prose chopped up into lines of varying lengths. Good prose depends on clear meaning, but not good poetry: that goes beyond meaning and depends for its magic on the associations and sounds of words. 'Domicile' and 'home' both mean places to live but they conjure up very different images.

I clearly recall one revealing incident on a Sunday morning after Richard had gone to his chapel and I to my church. He came back excitedly waving a newspaper and said, 'Listen to this.' He read the Dylan Thomas poem 'The force that through the green fuse drives the flower'. When he had finished I asked him what it meant. He replied, 'I don't know, but isn't it beautiful?' The poem was in a copy of a now long-extinct newspaper, the *Sunday Referee*. I told the story to Paul Ferris, who included it in his biography of Richard only to dismiss it as 'nonsense', because that issue of the paper had been published ten years before. I never said or thought that Richard had bought the paper. I don't know where he got it, perhaps from old piles of his fish and chip newspapers. All I do know is that it truly happened.

It was my first awareness of Dylan Thomas, and it sparked an admiring appreciation that grew with the years. Little did I know then that ten years later, just before he left for America for the last time, Dylan would come to spend an evening with me, tell me he felt he had reached the end of his lyrical impulse, and ask for my help in writing a stage play, tentatively called *Two Streets*. Nor could I foresee that, a couple of months after his death, the three Burtons – Richard, Sybil and I – would take part in the London production of Dylan's radio play *Under Milk Wood*, with Richard playing the part Dylan had written for himself.

Of course, you can't learn acting in a living room, and I saw to it that Richard played to radio and theatre audiences. One notable radio experience occurred in an adaptation I had made of Francis Brett Young's *The House under the Water*. On the day before the broadcast in Cardiff the play was timed and was found to be five minutes short. That night I wrote an additional scene which was built around the character Richard was playing. We worked on it at home and it came off brilliantly.

But it was the theatre that was Richard's natural sphere. Here he had something that nobody could give him: stage presence. It's the quality that distinguishes the genuine star from the merely talented actor. It was remarkably demonstrated when Richard played the Bastard in the Old Vic production of Shakespeare's *King John*. The director had the seemingly good idea of letting the Bastard observe much of the action from the side of the stage, since he makes so many subsequent comments on it, but after a few performances it was clear that Richard was distracting the audience's attention just by being there, watching and listening. One of the most difficult things for a stage actor to do is to listen to dialogue he has heard a hundred times as if he were hearing it for the first time. I always taught Richard never to worry about what he should do on stage, but to concentrate on imaginatively being the character; being begets doing.

That silent stage presence of his lost him a job early in his career. It was in *Adventure Story*, a play about Alexander the Great. The leading man was Paul Scofield and Richard had been cast as his friend, Hephaestion. Incidentally, Paul and Richard became good friends. But in that play it was soon decided that Richard's silent presence on the stage was too distracting.

While he was at school I gave him every chance I could to play before an audience, both in the school itself and in the local YMCA. He loved performing. When he first came to live with me he showed some envy of his younger brother Graham's success as a soprano in the local eisteddfodau, the Welsh competitive festivals. I pointed out that his voice had certainly ceased to be soprano, but he pestered me to teach him the solo for the next eisteddfod. It was Sullivan's 'Orpheus with His Lute'. One evening I reluctantly agreed to go back to school and attempt to teach him the solo. (I was the pianist for the school assembly, which took place every morning.) The piano was on the platform of the assembly hall and parallel to the side walls. Richard faced the non-existent audience and so couldn't see my reaction as he gave vent to excruciating sounds. At last I could contain my laughter no longer. He turned to me in dumbfounded fury. Then he stalked out angrily, exclaiming, 'I'll show you. Someday I'll show you.' And he did. On the first night of *Camelot* on Broadway, on 3 December 1960, I went into his crowded dressing room after the performance and he greeted me with, 'Well, I showed you, didn't I?' I didn't know what he was talking about; he explained later.

I suppose his greatest acting achievement while at school was as Professor Higgins in Bernard Shaw's *Pygmalion*. Could a seventeen-year-old boy striving to lose a strong Welsh accent be sufficiently convincing as an expert in English speech? He was. So thoroughly did we get rid of his native accent that ultimately, when he told a story with a Welsh setting, the accent became falsely exaggerated. But he always welcomed an opportunity to speak in the Welsh language.

I taught Richard to be subconsciously aware of his audience. That will sound like heresy to a strict adherent of the Method school of acting, in which, it seems to me, an audience tends to become an intrusion on a private rite. Yet it's the audience that makes the play a living experience. The words the actor says every night are the same – or should be! – but no two audiences are the same, and that ensures that no two performances are the same. By teaching Richard to be aware of his audience I did not mean that he should play to them, not even in a soliloquy; the concentration of the actor must always be on the character he is playing. The only time he must directly play to the audience is when his function is that of a narrator, such as the Chorus in Shakespeare's *Henry V*. When I taught Shakespeare to a class of established professional actors, I always started with the Chorus so that there was no complication of character or situation; we concentrated entirely on capturing the audience's attention and conveying a meaning in an unusual form of speech, Elizabethan blank verse.

An innate awareness of an audience is an essential check on an actor's work; that alone will guarantee the vitality of his performance. His private life is bound to impinge at times, and a bad day may well result in a bad performance; but an audience can help prevent this if the actor is sufficiently conscious of its presence. Richard had a magical rapport with his audience. He never forgot my dictum: 'Always remember that your hundredth performance is their first.' The magic moments for an actor or an orator are those when he induces a thousand people to be held in a silence that can be felt.

In comedy, of course, all actors are acutely aware of the audience's reaction. When a never-failing laugh line fails to get even an audible chuckle, many actors immediately think, What's wrong with them? What they should ask is, What's wrong with me? Of course, audiences vary enormously, each having its own conglomerate personality. Those who have paid large sums for a charity performance are very different from those enthusiasts who have waited perhaps months for a gallery seat.

On occasions Richard used his sensitivity to an audience to

increase their enjoyment. In the original Broadway production of *Camelot* he sang a duet with Julie Andrews, 'That's What Simple Folks Do'. I had told him that when something goes visibly wrong on the stage the audience is often aware of it before the actors, and a sensitive actor will feel their embarrassment and/or amusement. The actor then should surreptitiously find out what's wrong and, when he does, he should let the audience sense that he knows what the trouble is. Then embarrassment will change to excited expectation: what is he going to do about it? One night Richard sensed that something was wrong, and from the corner of his eye he saw that the stage hands had raised the backcloth and left it halfway up, exposing the brick wall of the theatre. Richard turned his head and deliberately looked at it, and then resumed the duet. As they sang the last line, 'That's what simple folks do', he pointed to the back wall at the word 'That's' and offstage at 'simple folks do'. It has become a treasured memory for those who were in the audience.

Acting in films could never satisfy Richard as the theatre did; the film is the director's medium. What artistic satisfaction can an actor get from doing several times perhaps a minute of the film out of sequence? Of course, it calls for tremendous concentration of the mind and the imagination. No one was more aware than Richard of the worthlessness of several of the films he was in, and very rarely would he consent to see even the good ones. There are moments, fleeting ones fortunately, when an intelligent actor – and Richard had a very good mind – despises his craft. Richard's respect was for the writer, and there were times when he longed to be one. I suppose it is human to undervalue what has become easy for us, and to wish for another talent.

During the time Richard lived with me I tried not to interfere with his private life, but he had very little free time because he was always most eager to work with me. Two revealing incidents stand out in my memory. I had become completely responsible for him financially. I had not had an easy life because I had virtually fended for myself from the age of fourteen when

25

my father had been killed in a mining accident. It was not surprising that money was a major preoccupation of mine, but to counter this obsessive concern I would sometimes make an extravagant purchase. I once bought a raincoat for Richard, far more expensive than any I had ever possessed myself. Proudly he wore it one evening – and lost it, in a billiard hall!

I never inquired about his activities on his evenings out; but on one such evening he forgot to take his key, and he came back after everyone was in bed. The next day he told me that he had gone to the back of the house and tried to wake me by throwing pebbles up at my window. He had been warned never to disturb the engineer, whose bedroom was between his and mine. He failed to wake me and gave up any hope of getting to bed that night. He had spent it in a cemetery on the bank of a stream, the Ffrwdwyllt, the Wild Stream.

My squadron (499) of the ATC became very successful, so much so that I was awarded a national honour, the MBE (Military), which stands for Member of the British Empire. I mention this because it put me in favoured touch with the Commanding Officer for Wales, and through him I was able to gain admittance for Richard to Exeter College, Oxford, for six months prior to his joining the RAF, a privilege granted to very few cadets. If they made a good impression during that brief stay at the university, they would be given priority for consideration as undergraduates when they were demobilized. But the Commanding Officer brought up an important issue: the ambiguity of my relationship to Richard. He had another home and his father was still alive; it would be better and easier all round if I adopted him. When I raised the question with Richard he readily agreed to become my adopted son. I put the matter in the hands of a local solicitor, and he took it up with the magistrates. I was well known locally and they met with no objection to the adoption. But when it was discovered that I was twenty days short of being twenty-one years older than Richard, legal adoption was ruled out. The alternative was that Richard become my legal ward, and for that his father's signed agreement was necessary. David Jenkins, a brother of Richard and a police officer, undertook to secure this and did so with no difficulty. Richard's name was then changed by deed poll to Burton. Gradually the teacher–pupil relationship became one of father and son, and in later years he always referred to me as his father. He told me that when he heard in 1957 that his father was dead, his immediate reaction was 'Which?'

The change in our relationship is well documented by his inscriptions on the first three gifts he gave me, all of them books of poetry. The first, the *Collected Poems, Epistles and Satires* of Alexander Pope, reads, 'To P.H.B. on the occasion of my first R.A.F. pay, July 23rd 1943, when I was attested at Penarth. Richie'; the second, A.E. Housman's *A Shropshire Lad*: 'To Phil out of my first B.B.C. cheque. August 13th 1943. Ritchie [sic]'; the third, Hilaire Belloc's *Sonnets and Verse*: 'To Phil from his other half. Richie. November 30th 1945.' That last one was for my forty-first birthday.

CHAPTER
Three

Unlike the great majority of British actors in those days, Richard did not find his way to London's West End theatre by the usual provincial repertory route; he went there directly, when he was eighteen. Emlyn Williams had written a play with a Welsh setting, *The Druid's Rest*, and he and Daphne Rye came to Cardiff to audition actors for the parts of two young brothers. We saw an advertisement for the auditions and decided that Richard should try for a part. It was comically ironic that he had worked hard every day for months to acquire standard English speech for the London stage, and now he had to regain his Welsh accent for his first part on that stage. He did regain it and was engaged, but for the smaller part of the elder brother; he was too old for the larger part. Nonetheless he was noticed when he made his London stage debut; one reviewer said that he showed 'exceptional ability'.

That audition in Cardiff brought him more, much more, than his first professional stage part. It brought him – and, incidentally, me too – a rewarding and abiding friendship with the author. It was very appropriate that it was Emlyn Williams who presided over the memorial gathering for Richard in London in 1984.

Emlyn gave Richard not only his first part on the London stage but also his first film part. It was in *The Last Days of Dolwyn*. Like my radio play, *The House under the Water*, in which I had written a last-minute extra scene for Richard, it dealt with the imminent drowning of a Welsh village to provide a reservoir for an English city.

The Last Days of Dolwyn gave Richard not only his first film part, a Welsh one, but also his first wife, a Welsh one, who became the mother of his two daughters Kate and Jessica. Sybil too had stage and film ambitions, but when she married she found her fulfilment in her family and in supporting Richard's career. She is a wise and delightful woman, and we became closely bound together in our shared concern for Richard and the children.

At that first meeting with Emlyn Williams in Cardiff, Richard also met Daphne Rye, who was representing the producer of the play, Hugh Beaumont. She had a wide knowledge of all aspects of the London theatre, and she too became a valuable friend to Richard, so much so that part of her house became the first London home of Mr and Mrs Richard Burton.

The Druid's Rest did not have a long run, and in April 1944 Richard began his six months' residence at Exeter College, Oxford. There too the greatest benefit he derived was from a personal contact which developed into an enduring friendship. It was with Professor Neville Coghill, a gracious and learned gentleman who had a passion for theatre. It was wartime and the well-known and much-respected Oxford University Dramatic Society, or OUDS, was in limbo, but Professor Coghill had been largely responsible for the formation of a temporary society, The Friends of OUDS. The immediate project at the time of Richard's arrival was an open-air production, in the cloister quadrangle of Christchurch, of Shakespeare's *Measure for Measure*. Although the play had already been cast, Richard got a small part. Then something happened – I can't remember what it was – and suddenly he was playing one of the leads, Angelo. He immediately got in touch with me in Port Talbot and implored me to come up for the weekend. I managed to do so and was very happy to meet Neville Coghill, who arranged for me to stay at the college. Then occurred a procedure that was to be repeated several times in the following years, whenever he was in trouble with a worthwhile part: we worked on it line by line, hour after hour, into the early morning. That night I saw the result; his performance amazingly incorporated all we had worked on. I never ceased to be astonished by how quickly and thoroughly he absorbed notes I gave him.

He had to go to a party after the show and I went to my room, eagerly waiting to share in his success. The hours passed but there was no sign of Richard. The college gates were locked. I began to get really worried; sleep was impossible for me. At last he came in, looking a mess. He had stealthily climbed over a wall – or was it a fence? – that was topped with barbed wire, and it had wrecked his trousers and bloodied his legs. His story was that he had fallen asleep on a couch as a result of our hours of intensive study followed by a nerve-racking performance. Even then I had a suspicion that too much alcohol had induced the sleep.

Among the people who saw Richard's Angelo was the all-powerful producer Hugh Beaumont, known to the theatre world as 'Binkie'. He had seen Richard as the Welsh boy in *The Druid's Rest*, but what a change was here! In speech, for instance. And how could the boy from that earlier play transform himself so successfully into a complicated and tortured adult, Angelo, in a matter of weeks? Beaumont was so impressed that he saw him at the end of the performance and told him that, when Richard was demobilized from the RAF after the war, he would give him a contract.

Richard was finally called up, and was soon sent to Canada to complete his training as a navigator; he was very disappointed that it was not as a pilot. The *Aquitania* took him across the Atlantic, as it had me in 1939.

The war in Europe was over just after he arrived in Canada; he was stationed in Halifax, Nova Scotia. He had heard me speak of the Baruths, my friends from my 1939 visit to the USA, and decided to visit them when on leave; he had their address in New York City. He set out with a pal, Dai 'Digger' Evans, both of them in uniform. I believe he told me that they hitchhiked most of the way; they certainly arrived without any money. When they got to the apartment on Claremont Avenue they discovered that the Baruths were in Vermont. (They had bought a farm there, in Waitsfield, and during the war years they housed older pupils from Alfred's school, who helped the local farmers in the wartime effort to increase production. After the war the farm was turned into a summer theatre school, and for a few summers I served as a teacher, coach and director. I was on the staff of the BBC at the time, but I was willingly given the necessary leave of absence because it enabled me, with the help of the BBC office in New York City, to make some radio documentaries about American life. It was difficult, if not impossible, for the BBC in those immediate post-war years to get the necessary dollars for such projects.)

Richard found that the Baruth apartment was occupied. They had arranged that a teacher of one of their daughters should have it for the summer. She called the family in Vermont. Alfred said he would send money to enable the two young men to travel by train to Vermont. While waiting for the money Richard and Dai Digger stayed in the apartment. Their first acquaintance with Manhattan was as penniless sightseers.

In speaking to Charlotte Baruth forty years after the visit of the two young men, I discovered her dominant memory was her admiration for Dai Digger, chiefly because of the way in which he unobtrusively looked after Richard, who all his life was able to find such necessary aides and companions.

They stayed in Waitsfield for two weeks. By then their leave was running out, and Alfred drove them hurriedly to Toronto, accompanied by Charlotte and her daughter Peggy, who was only six months younger than Richard. In the rush to get aboard the train to Halifax, Richard somehow or other took with him Peggy's coat! It was returned but I have a shrewd suspicion that it was Dai Digger who did the packaging and posting.

Shortly after that trip to the USA Richard's unit was shipped back to England, where their first base was in Norfolk. It was another two years before Richard became a private citizen again. I had moved to Cardiff after the war and become Features Producer at the BBC, which meant that I was in charge of dramatized documentaries. Cardiff now became Richard's home. Again we were fortunate in our landlady. We had a two-bedroom flat in the home of another delightful widow, Mrs Morris.

But my first memory of those later RAF days is not of Cardiff, but of Stratford-upon-Avon. In the summer of 1946 Richard had a leave which I used to take him to Stratford for the first time. I have no recollection of the plays we saw at the Memorial Theatre, but I do recall the hours we spent dreaming of when he would tread that stage. We stayed in a large private house with rooms let for summer visitors. During the afternoons when there was no matinée, all the visitors were out sightseeing, and we assumed we could use the back garden to work together in privacy. Our project at the time was Marlowe's *Doctor Faustus*, particularly the wonderful final soliloquy. (It might have been one of the plays we saw that season.) We didn't know that we had an unseen audience, the owners of the house. Some years later when Richard had become well known, they wrote a book in which they made laudatory reference to what they had seen and heard.

My other memory is set in Cardiff in the spring of the following year. I had written a dramatic documentary called *The Rescuers*, about Welsh miners trapped by a fall of roof in a coal mine. Richard was given leave of absence to play the part of the chief rescuer. Both of us felt very deeply about the subject matter; Richard because he had, and always kept, a family sympathy with the Welsh miner, and I because my own father had been so trapped. In his case, a second cave-in foiled the efforts of the rescuers. That broadcast became one of my few truly memorable ones.

When Richard was a civilian again, in November 1947, he reported to Hugh Beaumont as he had been invited to; thereafter he was rarely out of work, and sometimes did too much.

I moved to London in 1949 to become the Chief Instructor in the BBC Training Department. That was the year in which Richard married Sybil, a very happy event in my life. They bought a house in Hampstead, and soon I had a flat close to them. I followed every step in Richard's career, and treasured such notices as this one from the film *Now Barabbas Was a Robber*. It was written by the most notable film critic of the day, C.A. Lejeune. 'Mr. Burton, in particular, is an actor whose progress I shall watch with curiosity. To my mind, he has all the qualities of a leading man that the British film industry badly needs at this juncture: youth, good looks, a photogenic face, obviously alert intelligence, and a trick of getting the maximum effect with the minimum of fuss.'

My chief professional association with Richard was when he played Shakespeare; that priority had been there from the beginning. When we studied a character I deliberately stressed those traits that were naturally Richard's; thus he could never be convincing as a weakling. His first big opportunity, and it was an unexpectedly wonderful one, came in 1951 at the Memorial Theatre in Stratford-upon-Avon, when he was chosen to play Prince Hal in *Henry IV, Parts 1 and 2*, followed by the King in *Henry V*. My conception of the role, especially since we were seeing its full development in the three plays, was that even in his wild days the Prince must sometimes have been aware of the burden of kingship that lay ahead. There was one moment of which I was particularly proud, which occurred in *Henry IV, Part 1*. Falstaff and the Prince are having a high old time, both pretending in turn to be the King chastising Hal for his association with Falstaff. At the end Falstaff pleads with Hal as the King never to banish Falstaff: 'Banish plump Jack, and banish all the world.' I wanted Richard to take a moment to let the words have their full impact on the Prince, and then to say to himself, 'I do, I will.' And inevitably he does when he becomes king. His ultimate dismissal of Falstaff was the hardest task the new King had to perform, but he softened it with a promise:

> For competence of life I will allow you,
> That lack of means enforce you not to evils,
> And, as we learn you do reform yourselves,
> We will, according to your strength and qualities,
> Give you advancement.

Richard told me that his interpretation of Prince Hal got him into trouble with the director, who was himself playing Falstaff and consequently wanted no serious note to disturb the comedy of the tavern scenes.

I was deeply gratified by a notice written by Ken Tynan: 'A shrewd Welsh boy shines out with greatness. His playing of Prince Hal turned interested speculation to awe almost as soon as he started to speak; in the first intermission the local critics stood agape in the lobbies. Burton is a still, brimming pool, running disturbingly deep; at twenty-five he commands repose and can make silence garrulous.'

Some entries from my small diary express my joy at Richard's success in that 1951 Stratford season:

> Sunday, April 8th. [In London.] A quiet day at home, luxuriating in Rich's Stratford notices; they are miraculous.
> Friday, May 11th. Saw *Henry IV, Part 1*. Rich was magnificent and Sybil delightful. [Sybil had the small part of Lady Mortimer, who speaks only in Welsh. Shakespeare doesn't even give her speeches in an English translation.] This is bliss indeed.
> Saturday, May 12th. Am ecstatically happy. Gave Rich some notes in the morning, but nothing fundamental. *Henry IV, Part 2* in the evening. Rich still wonderful but a little uncertain in opening scenes because of the production.
> Sunday, May 13th. Whit Sunday. Another glorious day. Gave Rich notes in the morning, but the production will prevent him from doing much about the most important ones.
> Monday, May 14th. A doleful day. I had very reluctantly to leave Stratford after an idyllic weekend. I don't want a bit to go to America now.

But I did go to America and so I didn't see the climax of the series, *Henry V*, until . . .

> Saturday, September 22nd. Up early to go to Stratford. Rich and Syb met me at the station. Saw *Part 2* at the matinée; it is much better; 'Oh, polished perturbation' soliloquy

particularly impressive. Very moved in the evening by *Henry V*; there's no doubt about R's greatness. I feel proud, humble, and awed by God's mysterious ways.

Sunday, September 23rd. Reluctantly left Stratford. Missed the train but R. took me to Leamington, where I had to wait an hour. With R's encouragement have almost made the great decision to leave the BBC, probably at the end of next March. I'm growing to the inevitable.

The inevitable was that I belonged to the theatre.

Sunday, October 20th. A wonderful day. Rich went all out for me. The 'polished perturbation' scene probably better this afternoon than ever I shall see it, and in the evening the 'Once more unto the breach' speech was absolutely thrilling.

But the season was not entirely a success for Richard. He also played Ferdinand in *The Tempest*. It was too bland a part for him; all that was needed in the actor were good looks and a pleasing personality, whereas Richard required a more complex character. He wasn't happy playing Ferdinand, but I didn't think he was as bad as he thought he was. On the day I saw it, the note in my diary has one very surprising comment:

Saturday, September 15th. Quite enjoyed *The Tempest*. Rich's Ferdinand was good, but lacking in poetry.

Lacking in poetry? His contempt for the part must have expressed itself in robbing it of its lyricism. Three years later he was in an Old Vic production of the same play, but then he played Caliban. I myself was employed in the theatre by then, and I did not work with him on this part. I saw the play at a matinée, and noted in my diary that he was 'a good but lightweight Caliban; it's not a part to relax in'.

I had left the BBC on 29 February 1952, with a standing invitation to return if I should change my mind. On that extra leap-year day in my diary I wrote, 'Deep down I never thought I should have the courage to burn my boats. How much will I have accomplished before I come to this page again?' As it turned out, by 29 February 1956 I had already been settled in the USA for well over a year.

In my first year of freedom I sustained myself by my writing, which included the first twelve episodes – it was my decision to do no more – of a new television series, *The Appleyards*; however, I also spent five months in the USA, chiefly helping the Baruths at their summer theatre school in Vermont, and making another radio documentary for the BBC. When I was in London I saw a great deal of Richard and Sybil, and was very excited by Richard's performance in Lillian Hellman's *Montserrat*, which I saw both at the first night of the try-out in Brighton and at the first night at the Lyric Theatre in Hammersmith some two weeks later. My diary comment on the London opening reads: 'Richard had a tumultuous reception and made a delightful curtain speech. . . . Had a late and wonderful post-mortem with R. and S.'

My main project for the year was a very private one: to write a play for Richard. But I never even mentioned it to him; I wanted to surprise him with the finished script. The title was *The Dark Wood*, from the opening of Dante's *Inferno*: 'In the middle of our life's journey I awoke to find myself in a dark wood where the straight way was lost.' One of the big disappointments of my life was that he never played it, although I had seen and heard him in it as I wrote it.

Saturday, December 13th. A remarkable day's work on *The Dark Wood*; I was so stimulated by it that I went to bed in a whirl of phantasies and failed to get to sleep until 3 a.m.
Sunday, December 14th. Another remarkable day. It's an unequalled experience to get lost in a work of lonely creation. But oh! the agony of forcing oneself to get down to it.

Richard was now becoming known in the USA, and his film commitments prevented him from taking on the part I had written for him. While making his first American picture, *My*

Cousin Rachel, he received an offer to play the lead in the first-ever Cinemascope film. *The Robe*. Hollywood had got him, a fact that I often regretted, as did Richard. I suppose that once you've got into that international spotlight and on that money train it's hard to revert to the world that took you there, but sometimes Richard did revert to it and some of his most memorable theatre work still lay ahead. His artistic values didn't change; he was only really happy playing Shakespeare before a live audience.

As for *The Dark Wood*, without Richard in the leading role I lost interest in it. But it didn't die. On 1 March 1953, St David's Day and the tenth anniversary of the day Richard had first come to live with me, the BBC broadcast a television version of the play. I didn't get involved; it was Richard's play and he wasn't in it, and my diary records that I had strangely little interest even in watching it. Yet I could not but be gratified by the generally favourable reaction both of the press and the public; *The Critics* made it the subject of their weekly radio programme. I was inundated with telegrams and letters, and there were several inquiries about the rights from film companies. An American producer took an option on it for Broadway, but subsequently he asked me to rewrite it with an American setting. This I couldn't do: for me its setting in a Welsh steel town like Port Talbot is essential. Years later I did try to do the American rewrite but it didn't ring true to me; one of the central characters – not Richard's part – is a Communist trade-union leader, and there was no such person in the USA; I doubt that there is in Wales now.

In 1957 I directed a summer tour of Bernard Shaw's *Back to Methuselah*. James Daly was in the cast, and some friends of his came to see the play in Westport, Connecticut. Jim asked me to meet them after the performance. They had just returned from England and were full of the shows they had seen. They had also been impressed by a television play. As they described it – they hadn't mentioned the title – I suddenly blurted out, 'But I wrote it!' Only later did I receive a contract and payment from the BBC for the telefilm repeat of the original 1953 production of *The Dark Wood*.

I had sent a copy of the completed script to Richard in Hollywood, and on 17 March 1953, sixteen days after the successful television production of the play, I received a letter from him, expressing his enthusiasm for the role I had created for him and which he was never to perform.

CHAPTER
Four

I had spent the Christmas of 1952 in Wales and on Christmas Eve had received a telegram from H.M. Tennent (Hugh Beaumont) offering me a part in their 'Coronation All-Star' production at the Savoy Theatre of Oscar Wilde's *A Woman of No Importance*. I had accepted by telegram and thus, at the age of forty-eight, I entered the world to which I felt I belonged, the London professional theatre. I still remember how, as I drafted my acceptance, I smiled at the thought that the coronation of Queen Elizabeth II should be celebrated with a play bearing such a title.

A Woman of No Importance was indeed a star production. There were four of them in the cast: Clive Brook, Isabel Jeans, Athene Seyler, Nora Swinburne. The supporting cast had such well-known names as Jean Cadell and Aubrey Mather. But I was making my first appearance in a London theatre, and this belied the proclaimed all-star quality of the company. The physical production was breathtakingly elegant and costly. That, combined with the expense of the stars, caused it to be rumoured that if every seat at every performance in the Savoy Theatre had been sold, H.M. Tennent would still have lost money, and that Hugh Beaumont knew this. It was for him the tribute of the London theatre to Queen Elizabeth II on her coronation. The loss would be covered by the several successful productions he had running in the West End.

We opened on Thursday 12 February, and to general surprise the critical reaction was mixed; there was no out-and-out enthusiasm. The company had promised to stay together for at least a year, but now there was doubt whether the production would be alive to grace the great day, 2 June. In fact it survived until 1 August, after 179 performances in the West End, followed by two weeks in suburban theatres at Streatham Hill and Golders Green.

Richard got back from Hollywood in time to see it. He arrived home on 16 June and he and Sybil attended the play on the 18th. Afterwards they gave a wonderful party for the company at the Casanova. Sybil had first seen the show a month before; she had come home early to get their place ready for Richard's return, which had been delayed.

When I wrote to Richard about my first role in a London play, and one with such a distinguished company, he sent me a long cable expressing his delight at what he saw as my first step towards directing in the London theatre. I thoroughly enjoyed my London stage debut, particularly the fellowship of the company; most important was my friendship with the director, Michael Benthall, who was also to direct Richard later that year in his first appearances at the Old Vic, when he triumphed both as Hamlet and Coriolanus.

Even though I had but a small part in *A Woman of No Importance*, that of Mr Kelvil, MP, I thoroughly enjoyed the daily routine of going to the theatre. It became an escape from a too-busy day, for I continued to do a great deal of writing for the BBC. Another form of escape was the cinema, and I went to see Richard's first three Hollywood films: *My Cousin Rachel*, *Desert Rats* and *The Robe*. Whatever reservations I had about the films, I had none about Richard. My diary records that when I saw *Desert Rats* on 24 April I was 'overwhelmed with tearful pride'.

My being in London enabled me to work in depth with Richard on his Hamlet. I was sent the script of the cut version that was to be used, and on 30 June we began work. We had seven sessions, some of them long ones, all in my apartment, the last taking place on 9 July. Rehearsals started shortly thereafter, but I attended none of them.

The first performance was at the Edinburgh Festival on Monday 24 August. Since *A Woman of No Importance* had closed, I was free to be present at it. I had arrived the day before and my diary says I was relieved to find Richard 'at ease, happy and confident'. The performances were in the Assembly Hall and on a thrust stage. I had a front-row seat but it was on the side, and so I couldn't see his face during his soliloquies. My diary records, 'I was badly placed and my frustration neutralized my emotion, but R. is already for me a great Hamlet. We had a long and lovely session afterwards.' I saw the performance again two days later from a well-placed seat and was totally satisfied by it, so much so that I returned to London the next morning.

The first night at the Old Vic was on Monday 14 September. As a prelude to it, Richard, Sybil and I had had a most enjoyable lunch together. His performance that night was thrilling. Richard's Hamlet was a great success, as it was eleven years later on Broadway – on both sides of the Atlantic it had record runs – but it was a surprise to some critics and playgoers. They expected the introverted young prince called upon to commit an act of vengeful murder and yet restrained from the deed by a too-sensitive conscience. The supreme exemplar of that Hamlet is Sir John Gielgud, and the most famous literary expositor of it is Goethe. My conception of the character is diametrically opposed to this, and Richard's was completely the Hamlet I see. I have analysed this Hamlet at length elsewhere, but a brief summary seems necessary here.

To an Elizabethan like Shakespeare the ultimate crime was regicide, and Hamlet feels it his duty to commit that crime. Yet Claudius, however he came by the crown, is the anointed King. He himself says,

> There's such divinity doth hedge a king
> That treason can but peep to what it would,
> Acts little of his will.

And what grounds does Hamlet have for his act of revenge? The word of a ghost. Was it the spirit of his father, or an evil one tempting him to damn him?

> The spirit that I have seen
> May be a devil, and the devil hath power
> To assume a pleasing shape.

The crucial scene that challenges my concept of Hamlet is that in which he comes upon the King alone, apparently praying, when he is already fully persuaded of Claudius's guilt: 'Now might I do it pat.' Indeed he might. Then why doesn't he? *Hamlet* is a revenge play with a formula as fixed as that of a modern mystery play in which, at its best, the culprit proves to be the least suspected and the most convincing. In a satisfying revenge play the revenge must equal the crime, an eye for an eye and a tooth for a tooth. Never is a man more fit for death than when he is praying, as Hamlet perceived Claudius to be, but Hamlet's father had had no such preparation. Furthermore, had Hamlet killed the King then, the audience would have felt cheated because the revenge would have been based solely on Hamlet's solitary suspicion. As it turned out, it was completely justified because the King's guilt was publicly proclaimed before the whole court. 'The King, the King's to blame.' It is not Hamlet who says that, but Laertes. It's a perfect end to a revenge play. And let us not forget that the hyper-sensitive Hamlet incapable of action, to which audiences had grown accustomed, kills five men, three by the sword and two by diabolical cunning.

I'm not suggesting that Richard's Hamlet, which was mine, was right and Gielgud's was wrong. Far from it. Gielgud's Hamlet had been one of the most treasured experiences of my theatre-going, though I felt it was outshone by his own inimitable Richard II. Every actor reveals himself in every part he plays, but this is particularly true of Hamlet. One man's Hamlet cannot be another's, and so there was inevitable difficulty when Gielgud came to direct Richard in the play in 1964.

In addition to Hamlet, Richard played four other parts in the Old Vic season of 1953–54: Sir Toby Belch in *Twelfth Night*, the Bastard in *King John*, the title role in *Coriolanus*, and Caliban in *The Tempest*. Of these, we worked together on only two, the Bastard and Coriolanus. One day Michael Benthall called me up in great distress. Although it had long been announced that Richard would play Coriolanus, he had suddenly decided not to do so, and wouldn't budge; could I get him to change his mind? I said I'd try. Richard had not discussed it with me but I guessed what was wrong. He could find no jot of sympathy for the character, whose unmitigated contempt for ordinary folk was completely at variance with Richard's abiding identification with the working class. And there was no let-up in the character, not one soliloquy in which he questioned himself.

There followed a never-to-be-forgotten long night of discussion. I pointed out that it was Coriolanus's very lack of ambivalence that was admirable. However much we disagreed with his values, we had to admire his devotion to them. And he had no ulterior motive; he refused to benefit from his victories. He was a man of action, happy only in action. He had derived his heroic values from his mother, but she had taught him too well; in a moment that called for compromise she could do so, but her son couldn't. He was the quintessential soldier's hero.

Richard did change his mind, and with what a result! There's no such thing as a definitive Hamlet because he's such a multi-faceted character, but there is a definitive Coriolanus, and it was Richard's.

I kept an eye on Richard's performances from time to time, sometimes without letting him know in advance that I would be there. Thus my diary for 4 December says, 'To the Old Vic to see *Hamlet*. I was very worried by R's performance – absurdly sing-song and with incredible pauses – but he took my subsequent sermon very well.' Richard and I shared Shakespeare to such an extent that, when he was asked to write an article on 'What Shakespeare Means to Me', he asked me to do it for him; not that he couldn't have done it himself but the Old Vic season gave him no time. When he finally remembered about it, the deadline was so near that I had to dictate it, which I did to Valerie Douglas, Richard's personal manager for almost all of his career. She knew Richard as few did, his best and his worst; as in all of us there was a worst, but those who loved Richard readily forgave him.

On 8 January 1954, I was asked to meet the author, John Whiting, and the director, Frith Banbury, of a new play, *Marching Song*, which was about to go into rehearsal. I'm sure the meeting had been suggested by Daphne Rye, who had developed a friendly concern for my career in the theatre. As a result of the interview I was offered a small part in the play, but the chief reason for approaching me was to get me to understudy the main character part, Cadmus, which was to be played by Ernest Thesiger; they feared he wouldn't be able to stand the strain of a seven-city try-out tour. (Needless to say, he didn't miss a performance.)

Saturday, January 9th. Collected and read script of *Marching Song*. Am in a quandary, but am inclined to accept the part. Daphne thinks I am mad to hesitate.
Sunday, January 10th. Have practically decided to accept the part, gambling on the chance to play Cadmus.
Monday, January 11th. Phoned Sybil, but surprisingly it was R. who answered; his uninterested brusqueness was cruel.... He clearly won't be happy until I'm a big shot.... I said 'Yes' to the part.

Richard couldn't bear to think of me as a small-part actor. He had been happy about my being in *A Woman of No Importance* because it was such a distinguished production and I needed to get the feel of the London theatre, but once was enough. Our joint hope was that I would direct at the Old Vic, and Michael Benthall had given me some indication that this might happen the following season. Richard did come to see a matinée of *Marching Song*; he came backstage afterwards but said almost nothing about the play. Two weeks elapsed before he phoned me about it, but he had nothing good to say.

However, one thing I did made him very happy. On St David's Day it had become the custom to hold a big Welsh celebration in the Albert Hall in London, and I had been asked to plan and organize the programme for 1954. I did so, but the sad fact was that I couldn't be present for the event, which was highly successful, because I was in Blackpool, on tour with *Marching Song*.

Another event that year for which I had done a good deal of preliminary work, and in which Richard was involved, took place at the Old Vic on Sunday 7 March. It was a memorial to Dylan Thomas, who had died in New York City four months before. I had got to know Dylan very well and we had worked happily together. Although I hadn't been able to take part in the memorial I was able to be present at it because *Marching Song* was on its way from Blackpool to Bournemouth, and I had the intervening Sunday in London. What gratified me most about the evening was that it introduced Emlyn Williams to Dylan's work. Subsequently he asked me about him and became so interested in the subject that he varied his famous Dickens recitals with one devoted to Dylan.

Marching Song closed on 15 May after only forty-three performances in London; it deserved a better fate. The closure enabled me to see the hundredth performance of *Hamlet*; I noted that Richard 'gabbled a bit'. We had a delightful supper afterwards, with Sybil of course, and with Mr and Mrs Alec Guinness, and Mr and Mrs Robert Hardy. 'Tim' Hardy had been a friend of Richard's since their Oxford days, and I had got to know him well and always enjoyed his company.

On Friday 21 May my diary records, 'To *Coriolanus* in the evening. R. absolutely magnificent; this is true greatness.... The production is good, apart from the conception of the Tribunes.' The entry for 28 May records another exciting event: 'Up at 5.45 for a day in Shepperton Studios, filming "Pages from *Hamlet*". A historic day: the first production of the new Denham Films Ltd., and the first time Rich and I have worked together on a film. Apart from a 3-hours carpenters' strike, the day was happy and successful.'

On 29 May I wrote: 'The last night of the Old Vic season. R's fans nearly tore the place apart; he had to be smuggled away in a taxi. Ivor and Gwen came back with me and we had a worthwhile talk.' Ivor was an older brother of Richard, and Gwen was his wife. Richard was abidingly loyal to his brothers and sisters and their families, and was always a dependable source of help in time of need, but Ivor was the brother to whom he had been totally devoted since boyhood, because Ivor had been a local rugby-football hero and a coal miner. Ivor and Gwen had become an integral part of his immediate family – he had given them a house opposite his own in London, and they travelled with him everywhere; they had no children. Ivor's death years later would affect Richard deeply. The brothers spoke Welsh to each other, and this was always a happy bond between them. Richard told me that once, when they were in a bar in Geneva frequented by diplomats who conversed in a tangle of tongues, a gradual silence grew in the place as people became aware of a language being spoken that none of them knew. What secrets were they missing? That phrase in the diary, 'a worthwhile talk' refers to an ambivalence in Ivor's original attitude to me. What I shared with Richard he couldn't be a part of; as for me, I was concerned that Ivor was always too convenient a drinking partner for Richard, but gradually over the years an understanding and warmth developed between us. We realized that we were both necessary to Richard.

After *Marching Song* closed I was kept busy by the BBC, writing and directing, chiefly in Wales. There were no theatre prospects in London for the summer so I decided to spend it in America. Al Baruth had sold the farm in Vermont, but he still urged me to come. On Monday 12 July I had a wonderful Goodbye day with the family in Brighton. My diary says, 'Elfed met me at the station, a pleasant surprise. R. was in excellent form, and it was a memorable joy to see Cis, so beautiful, so relaxed, and so deeply happy.' Whenever I saw Elfed – and I had seen him and Cis in London a few times – my mind, and probably his, flashed back to that crucial scene in the front room of 73 Caradog Street, Taibach. 'You take 'im, Mr Burton. You take 'im.' Elfed was now a happy and carefree man.

The day before I set sail I had a farewell lunch with Richard and Valerie at the Acropolis. It looked as though we might be in the USA at the same time, but a continent apart. In fact Valerie arrived in New York five days after I did, and we had some pleasant days together, during which she got to know my friends Al and Charlotte Baruth. On one occasion I went with her to the Chrysler Building to meet Walter P. Chrysler, Jr and Lester Cowan. I suppose it was Cowan who arranged the meeting. He had some excellent credits as a Hollywood producer and was in the process of forming a new film company, Cowan-Chrysler Productions. The very next day he called Valerie to say that they wanted me to work for them as a writer.

Richard and Sybil arrived a week after Valerie. They were on their way to Hollywood where Richard was to make *The Prince of Players*, the story of Edwin Booth, the justly famous nineteenth-century American Shakespearean actor and the elder brother of John Wilkes Booth, also an actor but not famous as such. My diary has a sour note on Wednesday 4 August. 'A wonderful session with Richard and Al Baruth at the Players' Club. The script of *The Prince of Players*, which I read until 3 a.m., is an even worse disgrace after the wealth of material available in the Players' library.' (Edwin Booth had founded the Players' Club.) My estimate of the film script was equally true of the finished product.

After days of negotiation with Lester Cowan and Walter Chrysler, I finally signed a contract putting me in charge of their script department, with an additional contract whenever I wrote a film script. The delay was caused by the fact that I didn't want to commit myself beyond an experimental six months, while Chrysler insisted on a five-year contract. I reluctantly agreed to a three-year one, but then to my dismay the company itself dissolved in six months, and I was left without a job in a strange land. After much thought I decided to stay in America, and I have not regretted that final decision.

Bernard Shaw used to say that the way to ensure a healthy long life was to be seriously ill at forty; I was. I would add that the way to ensure a happy long life is to move to a place where you are not known and start all over again at fifty; I did.

CHAPTER
Five

My status in the USA was gradually changed from Visitor to Resident Alien, without the usual procedure of my first having to leave the country. My new employer accomplished the change without even involving me, except for a pleasant interview with an immigration official, but it was a year before my status was finalized.

I had suspected that one of Cowan-Chrysler's objects in employing me was to get ready access to Richard, whom they hoped to persuade to do a film for them; the first thing they asked me to do was fly out to Hollywood to discuss possibilities with him. I went for a week and had what my diary describes as 'a dream-visit'. While I was there, Richard was not too busy with *The Prince of Players*, but I did spend one day with him at the studios where he was doing various snippets of *Hamlet* as played by Edwin Booth. It seems I was impressed by 'a wonderful reconstruction of a period New York theatre, the splendour of Richard's dressing-suite, and the ineffable boredom of film-making for most of the myriads involved'.

Richard took full advantage of my being in Hollywood to introduce me to his friends, and I attended parties at the homes of Humphrey Bogart, George Cukor and James Mason. Valerie was so certain that Hollywood would become my home base that she took me to see a house she had picked out for me. Richard was responsive to the Cowan-Chrysler approach so that my visit was professionally justified, and when I got back I began work on a film script intended for him. I had not chosen the subject, and I had some doubts about its appeal to Richard. It was called *The Sea Devil* and was based on the life of the German maritime hero Count Von Luckner. In World War I he used a sailing ship flying the Norwegian flag as a disguised raider in the Atlantic, and sank forty ships without a single loss of life on either side; he may have been the last embodiment of chivalry in modern warfare. I finished the script very quickly. Both Cowan and Chrysler were enthusiastic when I read it to them, and it was sent to Richard. He read it immediately, a rare occurrence. He thought it was good, but not something for him – and that was the end of that. He was always, and rightly, more interested in complicated characters than in straightforward heroes.

Walter Chrysler, Jr was a well-known art collector, and my office in the Chrysler Building was such that people made excuses to come to see me – I mean, see it. The furniture was genuine Sheraton, and on the walls were paintings by, among others, Van Gogh (a self-portrait), Corot and Mary Cassatt. In the anteroom there was an El Greco, and in the main room of the suite a wonderful Madonna from Picasso's Blue Period.

Richard, Sybil and Valerie stayed six days in New York on their way back to London, and we had a delightful time together. They approved of the apartment I now occupied in the Beaux Arts, and I had a sense of being permanently left behind when they set sail on the *Liberté*, but the Baruths made me feel very much at home.

After the demise of *The Sea Devil* project my next task was to find a property that would interest Gina Lollobrigida. This took some time, but I finally came up with one that the star's representatives were very interested in. My job was to get the beautiful lady eager to do the film. For this a meeting was arranged in the elegant reception room of the Chrysler suite. Present were Miss Lollobrigida, her manager, agent and other advisers, Lester Cowan, Walter Chrysler, and myself. I outlined the story at considerable length with emphasis on the leading part, and my presentation was received with approving smiles and nods. When I finished, all turned to the final court of appeal. Her smiling response was simply, ''ow much?'

After four months with Cowan-Chrysler it became increasingly obvious to me that the partnership would dissolve, but it took them another three months to do so. Throughout that time I kept working on possible projects until it became absurd. Chrysler, because of his money, was the kingpin and he ultimately forbade Cowan to come to the office. Finally a settlement was made, and I was given a reasonable severance pay, half of which was to come from Chrysler and half from Cowan; I got only the first half. There could hardly have been a more ill-assorted pair than Walter Chrysler and Lester Cowan, although I liked both men and remained friends with them. Lester was always full of projects but few of them came to fruition. He continued to try to involve me in his plans and on occasions he partially succeeded.

After an agony of indecision during which I booked a passage home, I finally cabled London on 29 March 1955 to arrange to to give up my flat in Hampstead. The die was now cast, but I slept little. At the time Richard was in Spain, working on *Alexander the Great*, and I gathered from his letters and those of Valerie that things were not going too happily with the film. As to my own dilemma, at first Richard was non-committal about my decision to stay in America, but then, in a second letter, he approved of it. Thus our shared dream of my directing him in Shakespeare in the London theatre was finally shattered.

The summer was one of unfulfilled hopes. I was invited to work, and did, on several projects, but nothing came of anything. At Walter Chrysler's kind invitation I still used an office in his suite and we enjoyed a friendly association. Richard, Sybil and Valerie arrived from Spain in late July – they were on their way to Hollywood where Richard would make *The Rains of Ranchipur* – and Walter gave a cocktail party for them. With them this time were Ivor and Gwen, making their first visit to America; they found Manhattan to be rather overwhelming. On 29 July my diary records, 'Sybil revealed that R. is losing confidence in his ability. [This must have been a reaction to his difficulties in Spain.] I gave him a pep-talk and enthused about his doing *Othello* at the Old Vic in the coming season. We were very close.' Two days later I wrote, 'R's visit has made me put on 6 lbs!'

It was mid-August before I earned any money, when I got a small advance on a book I had written for a musical, *Las Vegas*. Two weeks after I officially became a Resident Alien, Richard surprised me by arriving in New York for a day. He was on his way to London for another season at the Old Vic. (The other members of his family had already gone home.)

I was sorely tempted to return to London for Richard's second Old Vic season, but to have done so would have been to admit failure in the USA, and I was besieged by inviting possibilities. Richard did only two plays at the Old Vic that season: *Henry V*, for which he received notices that even surpassed those of his original Stratford portrayal, and *Othello*, in which he alternated the parts of Othello and Iago with John Neville. According to the notices I read, Richard's Iago outdid his Othello, again the challenge of the more complicated character. I felt it to be a great deprivation not to have seen either. And how I wished I had worked with him on Othello! It was a part I myself had played in my long-gone amateur days.

For most of 1955 I was a freelance. I got to know lots of important people in show business, and was encouraged to work on several projects. This kept me happily and hopefully busy, but all my work ended in naught; and all the time there was an abundance of real work waiting for me in Britain. On 1 January 1956 my diary sums up: '1956 is almost bound to be more successful than '55, but it's surprising how happy I really was in '55.' A year later I wrote, '1956 fulfilled its promise. Now for 1957.'

I began 1956 by working informally with Robert 'Tim' Hardy, Richard's Oxford friend. He was making his Broadway debut in a play by Emlyn Williams, *Someone Waiting*, in which the leading part was played by an actor who had become a very good friend of mine, Leo G. Carroll. Tim knew no one in New York and so made contact with me soon after his arrival. Our shared memories of Richard did much to console me for not being in London; the quality in Richard that Tim always emphasized was his latent power, both on- and offstage. Tim's upbringing had been a privileged one, very different from Richard's; deeply cultured and intelligent, he was a truly dedicated actor. I enjoyed his company very much, and I introduced him to Sally, daughter of the actress Gladys Cooper, who invited us to a late supper in her apartment after an evening performance of *Someone Waiting*. The ultimate result of that happy late night was that Sally became the second Mrs Robert Hardy. It is now thirty-five years since Tim and I were in New York together, and it has gladdened my heart to hear from time to time of his continued success as an actor. He is best known in America for his part in *All Creatures Great and Small*.

My friendship with Walter Chrysler led to an unusual adventure that February. He had agreed to a touring exhibition, beginning in Portland, Oregon, of a hundred items from his treasury of fine art. They were to be conveyed in two large vans, whose load could be insured for only a third of its many millions in value. To avoid the northern winter weather, the route was to be through the south. It had been arranged that Walter Chrysler was to go in one van and I in the other, but at the last moment he had to stay in New York. The loading of the vans and the safeguarding of their contents required great expertise; it took about eight hours. I remember particularly the difficulty caused by one painting which was twenty feet long; when it was finally unloaded it was so baffling to the uninitiated that they didn't know which end was up. It was Monet's *Nympheas*.

This was the second time I had travelled by road the length and breadth of the USA, and its richness and variety, both in itself and in its people, did much to fortify my still uncertain resolve to stay there. The driver of my van was Dick Giglio, a friendly and lively companion. With him was a learner driver, Jerry Hutchins, a quiet and reserved contrast to Dick, but an equally good companion. We never saw the other van. I had to get what sleep I could on the floor alongside the *Nympheas*, while Dick drove on unrelentingly; his endurance was phenomenal. He was determined to get to his home in Anaheim,

California in time to spend a few days with his wife, Irma, and his three children before completing the journey. We actually had three days in California, and Valerie came to Anaheim to pick me up. I had a pleasant stay with her and her friends in Hollywood, but I took one evening off to take the Giglios to the Moulin Rouge; their enjoyment was very rewarding.

While I was in California, Valerie introduced me to a few people who were involved in a major plan for Richard about which she was very enthusiastic. We discussed some possible projects but my mind was more occupied with Richard's Othello, which was just opening at that time.

My diary records the end of the Portland trip thus: 'Sunday, February 12th. As soon as we hit the Oregon border we were under constant police surveillance. Deep snow, slushy and slippery roads, swirling mists created the most difficult hazards of the trip, but we made Portland by midnight.' Elaborate preparations had been made for the arrival of the paintings, and I found the excitement they created very moving. I myself was warmly welcomed but I stayed only two days before beginning the long train journey back to New York. I had wanted to see snow and now travelled through 2,000 miles of what seemed to be the Arctic waste. The welcome home by the Baruths was very reassuring, and this was reinforced the next day by a meeting with Walter Chrysler. But no good news awaited me professionally; I had been away just over two weeks.

Three days after my return I was greatly surprised by the appearance of Valerie, who was on her way to London. She had received a cable from Richard cancelling the plan about which she had been so enthusiastic. She was going to see him in the hope of changing his mind. She stayed in New York for two days and together we went to see *Someone Waiting*. To my surprise we found it to be disappointing; it was soon to close. I couldn't put my finger on what had gone wrong with the production. The next day a depressed but determined Valerie set sail for London. The failure of *Someone Waiting* meant that Robert Hardy soon went home, too, followed a few months later by Sally Cooper. During those few months I saw her fairly frequently, occasionally with her ever-beautiful mother.

I was much cheered on 1 March by a delightful anniversary cable from Richard with good news about *Othello*. Two weeks later came a happy letter from Valerie to say that Richard had changed his mind about the plan. Somehow those two messages typified for me the clash in Richard between theatre and films.

It seemed I always ended up teaching. I began my career in a secondary school without any prior training, and later became the Chief Instructor in the BBC Training Department. Now came an offer in New York City. It had been suggested that I get in touch with Sanford Meisner, a deservedly well-known teacher of acting. In addition to his work in the Neighborhood Playhouse School, he ran a late-night class for professional actors, and he invited me to give a series of talks about Shakespeare. For people deeply committed to the strictly naturalistic school of acting, Shakespeare presents almost insurmountable obstacles. In preparation for the class I would rehearse each week a scene from one of the plays. Here was something to keep me occupied.

During the year since Cowan-Chrysler had ceased to be, Lester Cowan had persistently kept in touch with me, always dangling the imminent prospect of my involvement in some fascinating project; he seemed determined to keep me in the USA. Occasionally he came through with a little of the money he owed me, and his friendship and that of his wife, Ann Ronnell, whose field was music, was a never-failing pleasure. At last, one of Lester's projects seemed to be coming to fruition: a film about Simon Bolivar for which I was to do the research and write the script. Shakespeare and Bolivar kept me happily busy. My immediate thought at mention of Bolivar was that it might be a good vehicle for Richard, but I hadn't been working long on it before I came to the reluctant conclusion that it was not a part for him. Lester had some important South Americans interested in the project, and I met and liked them. Subsequently, when Lester was out of town, they invited me to lunch. They wanted to sound me out about Lester because they felt he was stalling. It had long seemed to me that Lester's happiness was in planning; his elaborate refinement after refinement of project after project had finally soured Walter Chrysler and caused the break-up of Cowan-Chrysler. For selfish reasons I did my best to reassure the potential South American backers, as I had bolstered my own hopes, by emphasizing some of Lester's Hollywood achievements, notably *The Story of GI Joe* and *Tomorrow the World*.

The embarrassment of the Cowan-Chrysler disaster was renewed when I had to appear a few times at the arbitration hearings between the two members of the brief partnership. Then the sadly expected happened to the Bolivar project: Lester was having difficulties with one of the South Americans, a key man. But I had become so absorbed in the material that I continued work on it, and I was encouraged by receiving a token advance payment. I was much heartened, too, by an occasional long letter from Richard, who came to Jamaica that summer to make a film which proved troublesome and not worth the trouble: *Sea Wyf* (later, *Sea Wife*). When I saw the film I recorded that I was 'ashamed of his performance'.

Bolivar was not Lester Cowan's only project at the time. For a whole year he had been negotiating a big deal with NBC, from which he promised me great things. Then I heard from a confidential source that that deal too had come apart and that NBC was pressing for the return of an advance that had been made to Lester. I suppose he impressed people by his substantial Hollywood credits and his very imaginative proposals. When I heard of the NBC no-go, I had just delivered my third full report on Bolivar. Despite these frustrations, I was able to enjoy working individually with Mildred Dunnock and Kent Smith on parts they were playing in the American Stratford Shakespeare Festival. (Mildred became determined to get me invited to run the festival.)

My state of gnawing indecision again resulted in my booking a passage home and later cancelling it. A characteristic entry in my diary at this time reads: 'A long session with Lester, who gave me dreams for years ahead.' The trouble was that he couldn't let me alone to complete a piece of writing, and his constant pressure and interruptions resulted in some perfunctory work.

Shakespeare, as for most of my professional life, was my particular joy at this time because I had been persuaded to give a series of twenty lectures entitled 'Shakespeare for Actors' in Steinway Hall. I had had to bear all the initial expense of advertising and printing. Registration was slow, but forty-four people turned up for the first lecture and I completed the series to appreciative audiences. It was a good experience for me.

Things took a decided turn for the better in November when I was engaged to direct an off-Broadway production of Sean O'Casey's *Purple Dust* at the Cherry Lane Theatre. Noel Behn, the producer, had first approached me to play a leading part in the production, but I had persuaded him to let me direct it. This truly turned out to be a watershed for me.

During the ordeal of auditioning for the play, an ordeal because you have to say no to talented people desperate for work, I welcomed the chance for a few meetings with John Neville and his wife Caroline, who had come to New York. Naturally, the chief subject of our conversation was *Othello*, in which John and Richard had alternated the two chief parts. It brought Richard very near and did much to counter my disappointment at not having seen the production.

At that time actors in off-Broadway productions could not be given run-of-the-play contracts, and during rehearsals of *Purple Dust* we lost some members of the cast to television, but there was no dearth of replacements, and two were marked improvements. We even rehearsed on Christmas Day because we opened – triumphantly – on 27 December. Valerie saw to it that she was there so that she could report to Richard, and I'm sure she sent him the notices. He wouldn't read his own but perhaps he would read mine. Brooks Atkinson in the *New York Times* was particularly complimentary to me.

My conversation with Valerie was largely about a major move Richard was contemplating, one of which she heartily approved. Other British artists had set an example: to avoid excessive taxation in Britain, move to Switzerland and become a legal resident there. My instinctive reaction was to oppose this because it would take Richard away from the world in which he was at his best and happiest, the London theatre. For Valerie Richard's world was Hollywood, which existed to make big money, which should be protected by all possible means. Richard did make the move and bought a lovely but modest villa with ample grounds in Celigny, which is on Lake Geneva, some miles east of the City of Geneva. Inevitably he called his new home Le Pays de Galles.

In January 1957 I received the first letter from Richard written in his new Swiss home, and I was deeply disturbed by it; I described it in my diary as 'world-weary'. I think it sprang from perhaps a subconscious realization of the significance of the move he had made. In my reply I did what I could to reassure him, but I longed to see him, and was to do so sooner than I expected. In the meantime he was going to Libya to make a film, *Bitter Victory*. The best news I had was from Valerie, who was briefly in town: Sybil was pregnant. But Valerie had some bad news too; she must have had a difficult time with the world-weary Richard because she contemplated leaving him – fortunately she didn't.

I was very busy doing a variety of things: finding and rehearsing new actors as replacements in *Purple Dust*, which was a solid success (but the bigger the success the sooner did the actors in it get more lucrative offers); rehearsing scenes for Sanford Meisner's workshop; lecturing at Barnard College as a temporary replacement for Mildred Dunnock; and even making my debut as a television actor. Nevertheless in March I decided to go to Europe, but with no intention of staying there; such uncertainty was now over. I booked a return passage and was careful to get a re-entry permit. I said Europe rather than Britain because my primary purpose was to see Richard (I was to visit him and Sybil in Nice), but I would also visit friends in London and in Wales. I received a most welcome letter from Sybil, which did much to ease my mind about Richard. Of course, she was excited about the coming child; in my own way I was too.

Before leaving I attended a party to celebrate the hundredth performance of *Purple Dust*. I should be away for almost seven weeks, and I could not help but be worried about the show;

with the very probable certainty of new replacements, would it still be alive when I returned? And if it were, what state would it be in? Just before I set sail on 29 March I heard that one of the best actors in the company would be leaving in ten days. That intensified my guilt about abandoning the ship. All would now be in the hands of the stage manager, who would be rehearsing replacements and knew what I wanted. But what if *he* should leave for a better-paid job?

CHAPTER Six

The voyage was a pleasant one, including two enjoyable hours ashore in Bermuda. I had always been very susceptible to seasickness and had expected, as usual, to spend most of the time in my cabin, but to my infinite relief I was scarcely troubled, even though we ran into some rough weather. I think it was Bertrand Russell who said that the only advantage he had found in getting older was that you lost your tendency to seasickness. From my experience it seems that he was right. This enabled me to make some good friends on the voyage, most notably a dentist and his wife from Cleveland, Ohio, a friendship that endured until their deaths, many years later.

While waiting for a promised word from Richard – how often did I spend time in doing that! – I visited friends in London and Wales, and spent a day with Cis and her family. Sean O'Casey had urged me to visit him at his home in St Marychurch, which is near Torquay; he was eager to meet the director of the successful production of *Purple Dust*, which actually achieved a longer run than any other single production of one of his plays. During the visit, which was a great joy, I was surprised to learn that of all his plays his favourite was *Cock-a-Doodle Dandy*; that revelation was to bear fruit. Sean's political views were also unexpected: this gentle and compassionate man was ruthless in his Marxist philosophy. I understood later that his membership of the Communist party had prevented his getting a visa to come over to see *Purple Dust*.

I found at last that a letter from Richard was waiting for me in

London. It was written from the Hotel Negresco in Nice, where he and Sybil were having a holiday before returning to Celigny. I called the hotel and spoke to Sybil. She persuaded me to join them as soon as possible, and I did so the next day. They both met me at the airport; it was the beginning of a perfect weekend during which Richard convinced me of the wisdom of the move to Switzerland. More convincing than his arguments was his happiness.

I left on the Monday because I had to make another brief visit to Wales before sailing from Liverpool on the Friday morning. I was going back reluctantly because I had had so many happy reminders of my life in Britain, and because some eagerly awaited news from my agent in New York had not arrived, but I was considerably cheered to find that my Cleveland friends, Dr and Mrs Thomas, had changed their reservations in order to share the return sailing with me.

The day after my arrival in New York I went to see *Purple Dust*. I was relieved that it was still running, but was nonetheless depressed by the standard of the replacements; some of the other performances had also deteriorated. Even my right-hand man, the stage manager, had left. Still, the show was doing good business; how valuable the reputation of success can be!

On my return I was welcomed by some good news. I was to direct a cut version of Bernard Shaw's *Back to Methuselah*. It is a play in five parts, which had been cut in order to make one performance. The cutting had been skilfully done by Arnold Moss, who was himself in the cast, along with Celeste Holm; later James Daly joined us. The production was intended by the Theatre Guild for a summer theatre tour with possible transference to Broadway. So began some hectic weeks: working with the *Purple Dust* company and finding replacements for it, auditioning at the Theatre Guild, and revising the script of the Shaw play with Arnold Moss, whom I found to be very amenable.

The tour of *Back to Methuselah* opened in Saratoga, and Lawrence Langner and Armina Marshall, who were in effect the Theatre Guild, were so impressed that they decided to bring the production to Broadway. After staying with the play a couple of weeks I returned to Manhattan to begin rehearsals for a small-scale musical which I had agreed to direct. Soon after this had opened, I received a call from Celeste Holm to say that the *Methuselah* company needed me because it was losing confidence in the play itself. From the beginning I had been surprised by the choice of such a work for a summer theatre tour – it certainly was not relaxing entertainment – and much of the reviewers' praise had been for the production, not the play. A specially chartered Piper plane was sent to fetch me; I was to try to tune up the production for the important engagement in Westport. When I watched *Methuselah* on the evening I arrived, I found myself relieved by the performances, with one or two exceptions, but the audience reacted as if the play were in a foreign language; small wonder that the company had lost confidence in it. Then came the Westport opening night. My diary comment: 'A big disappointment. The physical set-up was bad and the company too keyed up. For the first time I lost heart and was ashamed to do so.' But I pulled myself and the company together the next day and, with the help of a major excision in the text, that evening saw the first of several good and well-received performances.

And what had become of Richard in the three months since I had seen him? Somehow I had got involved in complicated negotiations securing his release from his contract with 20th Century-Fox. In retrospect, I suppose I was hoping that it would free him for the theatre.

Back to Methuselah did good business at Westport, but when it closed on 30 August its rosy chances for transfer to Broadway had faded. Of course, as soon as I got back to Manhattan I went to see *Purple Dust*, which was much improved, but still in need of rehearsal. Within a few days I was auditioning for replacements again.

The great event that September was made known to me in a cable on the 11th: the baby had been born the day before, and all was well. Kate Burton, to whom this book is dedicated, had entered the world. The other welcome news in Richard's cable was that he was due to arrive the following day to begin rehearsals of Jean Anouilh's play *Time Remembered*: Sybil and the baby would be coming two months later. On 14 September I recorded: 'Wonderful meeting with R., our first alone for ages.'

Time Remembered, in which Richard appeared with Helen Hayes and Susan Strasberg, opened in New Haven in early October. I went to see it, but was not very interested in the play itself. I found that Richard, too, was unhappy with this lightweight comedy. Somehow or other he had to fit himself into an uncongenial production, and there wasn't much I could do to help him in that. I went back to Manhattan the following day because I was due to move into an apartment on West 67th Street, which was to be my home for seven years.

The Broadway prospects for *Back to Methuselah* were suddenly revived, but to enhance popular appeal Tyrone Power was to be the star. I met and liked him and the auguries were good for our working well together, but a premature announcement in the *Herald Tribune* that I was to direct the play caused some confusion because I was in preliminary negotiations to direct another play for Broadway. Much though I wanted to, I did not work on the new production of *Back to Methuselah*. Celeste Holm had some complication with the management and bowed out; she and I had become very good friends, and in loyalty to her I bowed out too. She accepted a part in another Broadway play, *Interlock*, and it turned out that I was to direct that. The author was Ira Levin, and it also starred Maximilian Schell. Arnold Moss was very distressed, and I felt bad too because I knew I had achieved something with the Shaw play; I wasn't happy about its coming to Broadway without me. It wasn't a success. Nor was *Interlock*.

On Saturday 9 November my diary records that I went to a Broadway preview of *Time Remembered*. 'The after-theatre party made the show seem even worse than it was. An almost imperceptibly drunken R. came back with me to my apartment. He was flooded with guilt.' Why did he feel so guilty? Partly because he was ashamed of my seeing him the worse for drink – he always tried to avoid that – but chiefly, I'm sure, because of the well-publicized affair he was having with Susan Strasberg. His guilt was intensified by the imminent arrival the following day – his thirty-second birthday – of Sybil and their two-month-old baby. Richard's brother David came too, and stayed through Christmas. It was my first sight of Kate, to whom I was to be 'Grandpa'. I went with Richard to meet them, and thus began the family's seven-month stay in New York.

During all the preliminary work for *Interlock* – Rosemary Harris had now joined the cast – I spent every available hour with my Burtons. I noted happily that my new role as Kate's grandfather served to strengthen my relationship with Richard. An otherwise happy Christmas Day was marred when Richard returned from the theatre that evening, already the worse for drink.

On 5 January 1958 *Purple Dust* finally closed after 430 performances; I attended the last night with mingled sadness and pride. I was aware that I owed the play a great deal. The rehearsals of *Interlock* did not go smoothly, chiefly because it was found that a good deal of rewriting was necessary, and Ira Levin, even though we had a good personal relationship, was not an easy author to deal with. Richard came to the final run-through in New York before our try-out in Wilmington, Delaware, and he was genuinely impressed; I'm sure his presence stimulated the company. The first night in Wilmington was quite exciting and went with surprising smoothness. Some very good reviews heartened us, but didn't prevent the usual second-night let-down.

We then moved to Washington, DC, where at a welcoming party given by Perle Mesta I experienced for the first time the ambassadorial set, as distinctive in its different way as the theatre set in New York. The glamorous opening of *Interlock* was a benefit performance; the show went very well but it was blasted by Richard Coe in the *Washington Post*, and depression set in. Coe's review was countered by some others but they didn't lift the pessimism. The producer, Richard Myers, rightly felt that some further drastic revisions of the text were urgently needed – I had failed to get them from the author, who has to approve all changes in his script – and Herman Shumlin was brought in to save the show. My name was to remain on the billing as the director, but I left the company in Washington. Shumlin managed to get some revisions made to the script but to no avail. *Interlock* opened on Broadway on Thursday 6 February and closed on Saturday the 8th.

I was curiously unaffected by having been part of a failure, and had an almost guilty sense of enjoyment at my freedom. Then there was the added delight of having the family in town. I saw a great deal of them, particularly Sybil. 'This time of failure could have been tough without them', I wrote in my diary. 'Thank God, too, for *Coriolanus*.'

A very exciting possibility had been born in talks with Richard: a film of *Coriolanus* set in South America in the nineteenth century. I suppose it was prompted by the work I had done on Bolivar. I set to work on the script at once, determined to use only the words of Shakespeare and those suggested by him, and in my excitement I finished the first draft in two weeks. Richard approved so heartily of what I had done that he wanted it typed at once (I always write in longhand; typewriters, like most machines, are beyond me) in order to send it to a producer who, he thought, would be interested. Two months later I noted, 'Some Wall Street tycoon has shown interest in the *Coriolanus* film', but ultimately the project, which would have been a very costly one, was indefinitely postponed for lack of funds. Occasionally in the following months there were signs of the problem's being solved, but it never was.

Among Richard's other professional activities during the run of *Time Remembered* was a television production of *Wuthering Heights* on 9 May. His Heathcliff was magnificent. He had arranged for me to see a preliminary run-through on the day before, so that I could give him some notes, and this I did in his dressing room at the theatre; few notes were needed.

On 19 May Sybil appeared charmingly with the eight-month-old Kate in a morning television show. It seems strangely fitting that twenty-six years later, by which time she had become an established actress, Kate should have partnered her father in his last television appearance.

Richard and I were both at this time in a quandary as to our next moves, the difference being that, while he was faced with several real offers, I had only vague possibilities dangled in front of me. Warner Brothers wanted Richard for a three-film deal. Having read all three scripts, I found myself in agreement with Richard, who was interested in only one of them: *Look Back in Anger*, from the play by John Osborne. Valerie came to New York and, as I expected, was very disappointed by Richard's refusal to sign the three-film contract. However, he did make *Look Back in Anger* in the autumn of that year, but in London. While it was not a Warner Brothers production, it was largely financed by them.

Time Remembered closed on 13 June. I had gone to see it again the previous evening. My diary comment: 'R. was much too conscious of my presence.' For my part I was much too conscious of the play's closing and the consequent departure of the family. Our farewell was marred by an incident in which both Richard and I were in the wrong. Let the diary tell the story.

> *Tuesday, June 17th*. The Farewell day. I took Kate out myself in the afternoon. . . . In the evening R. casually gave me a $50 bill. This annoyed me deeply as being ridiculous and demeaning. Foolishly I told Sybil my reaction, which angered her. I couldn't sleep after it.
>
> *Wednesday, June 18th*. I was very sad all day, largely because of my big mouth last night. I didn't even go to the ship; maybe I should have. Lost and fumbling, I went to the movies.

The next day I wrote a letter of reconciliation to await their arrival in Switzerland, and soon afterwards received a loving reply from Sybil.

Two days later came an offer to direct Sean O'Casey's *Cock-a-Doodle Dandy*, his favourite play. I wrote to him about it and got a charming letter back. Our try-out was to be in Toronto and, for some reason I have never understood, this lost us several actors I wanted. In fact we had great difficulty in casting the play, but finally assembled a good company, even though it was for an off-Broadway production.

The Toronto experience was a nightmare. Our excellent designer, Lester Polakov, had persuaded me to use a turntable on which to mount the set. In Toronto, this and the complicated lighting, for which the wiring was inadequate and resulted in black-outs, caused me to hold technical rehearsals until 5 a.m. But worst of all was the Roman Catholic opposition to the play, which was totally unexpected. It was demonstrated by noisy walk-outs, a furore in the press, Catholic protesters picketing the theatre, and ultimately in our having to have police protection. In spite of everything, the production showed promise, but we were all glad to get back to New York.

We had three weeks in which to get ready for the opening on 12 November. We used the time to good purpose, including simplifying the staging, but all was in vain, as witness my diary:

> *Wednesday, November 12th.* The great day ended in near disaster. A stuffy audience upset the cast. Even so, the show was good, but the critics panned it. The news came to an elaborate first-night party. I was very shaken.
>
> *Thursday, November 13th.* Today's papers continue the dirge. I don't understand it. My confidence is shaken. The company doesn't know what's hit them.

In this time of failure I was faintly tempted to return to the British Isles by a firm offer to take charge of a new commercial television station in Belfast, but a previous visit to that city, when I was on the staff of the BBC, had not enamoured me of it.

In spite of the notices, *Cock-a-Doodle Dandy* did run for two months, and would have run longer if the stage hands had agreed to a cut in pay; I didn't blame them for not doing so.

The last words in my diary for 1958: 'Oh, please, 1959!'

CHAPTER
Seven

Some letters from Richard and Sybil did much to lighten my depression, but I was so shaken by the failure of what I considered to be a good production of a very good, if unusual, play that I became instinctively sceptical about the quality of some of the plays I was offered to direct, even though I was longing for work. Then Richard arrived *en famille* on his way to Hollywood to make the films *Bramble Bush* and *Ice Palace*. Ivor and Gwen were in the party. The previous $50 difficulty was not mentioned, and being with them for a few days did me a lot of good.

While Richard was in New York I received my next directing contract for what seemed to be an exciting project: an off-Broadway festival of Bernard Shaw plays. The man behind it was an actor-turned-producer, Norman Roland. His choice for the first play was most unexpected: *Buoyant Billions*, which Shaw had written at the age of ninety-two. Being a Shavian enthusiast, I was excited about this. The theatre was to be the Provincetown and, musty though it was, this too excited me because of its association with Eugene O'Neill. The second play was *Getting Married*. I felt happily challenged to be doing little-known plays and to be working on them at the same time in repertory. The experience would be unusual for American actors, whereas it was customary in Britain.

Richard came to town for one day on his way to Maine to do some location work for *Bramble Bush*. He saw a preview of *Getting Married* and enjoyed it, but he couldn't wait to get back to my apartment for a talking session. He didn't even want to go out to eat; we made do with what I had. Rarely had I known him to be in the mood he was in that night. Normally he was very unsentimental; I knew his feelings for me, but that night he just had to tell me how much I meant to him, and it wasn't liquor that was speaking. Memories of that night did much to sustain me in a difficult time that lay ahead.

We had only small houses at the Shaw Festival previews, but their reactions were most encouraging. The first night of *Buoyant Billions* on 26 May had literally more press than public. This depressed me but the reviews were surprisingly good. However, business didn't improve. Then came the first night of *Getting Married* on 4 June. This time the notices were mixed, but Brooks Atkinson wrote a very supportive article about the Festival in the *New York Times*. And Norman Roland persisted in spite of poor houses; poor in quantity not quality. So absurdly, but admirably, unbusinesslike was he that he even added a third production to the Festival: two one-act plays, *Overruled* and *The Shewing-Up of Blanco Posnet*.

Between Richard's two films, he and the family came to New York in mid-June and stayed for a month, much to my joy. On the 19th my diary records that the 21-month-old Kate called me 'Grandpa' for the first time.

In spite of sparse audiences the Shaw Festival continued. I don't know how Norman Roland managed to keep it going. I helped as much as I could by giving several interviews about it on radio and television. As in all off-Broadway shows in those days, I was continually having to find and rehearse replacements for the cast. Sometimes it was difficult, particularly for character parts and during the summer, the time of maximum out-of-town employment for New York actors. I had great trouble in finding a replacement for the part of the General in *Getting Married* and, in desperation, decided to do it myself until I could get someone else. Richard wasn't able to come to see me, but Sybil and Gwen did, and seemed genuinely to approve of what they saw.

I read the script of Richard's next film, *Ice Palace*, and was disappointed. I described it as 'a cliché-packed story with travelogue trimmings'. When the family left for Hollywood again, they urged me to go with them. I couldn't do so straightaway, but I promised to join them as soon as possible and stay for a month. I found and rehearsed a replacement for me as the General and left for Hollywood on 29 July. To my surprise I was met at the airport by the whole family, less Kate. The house they had rented was delightful, and I began a most enjoyable and restful holiday in Lotos-Land – but I put on 9 lbs! Some of the location work for *Ice Palace* was to be done in Alaska, and Richard invited me to go with him; however, conditions there were reported to be rather difficult, so I declined. Richard left and was back in two weeks. It had proved impossible to carry out much of the shooting that had been planned. While he was away there was a scare one morning when Kate couldn't be found; she was later discovered in a lavatory in the grounds. On Richard's return from Alaska she was eager to show him where she had been lost and found!

While in filmland I read several scripts for Richard, but none I thought worthy of him. I did a fair amount of enjoyable socializing, and also agreed at the request of James Mason's agent to rework a film script, an adaptation of a novel, *Occasion of Glory*, to improve the part intended for his client. I took the script back with me to New York and did as I had been asked. I had assumed that the request had really come from the producer and the director. How naive of me! It turned out that those gentlemen were perfectly satisfied with the original balance of the parts. My weeks of work were unwanted and went unpaid.

The day before my return flight I was amazed by a call from Norman Roland asking me to add a fourth show to the Shaw Festival. It was to be *Candida* with *How He Lied to Her Husband* as a curtain raiser. I equivocated until I could see what the situation was; it was astonishing that the Festival was still running. When I got back I was relieved to find that the three shows were in pretty good shape, but business was still bad. How could Norman Roland keep them going? I managed to dissuade him from adding any more plays to the Festival, and soon thereafter it closed. It really had been an act of foolish daring to attempt any kind of theatre festival in Manhattan in the summer – and especially in a theatre where the air conditioning was unreliable! – but it was a very worthwhile project and, had the physical circumstances been different, I feel sure it would have been successful.

On 15 September I went with the producer, Michael Myerberg, who wanted me to work on another project of his, to see the American premiere of *Look Back in Anger*. Both of us were enthusiastic about it, but I was upset by the audience reaction. Almost a year before, Richard had written to me about the film and the initial response to it in London:

> The filming seems to have gone well tho' I know to my cost that there's many a slip twixt cutter and flick. Still, everybody is delighted with themselves, and I have had two letters from Tony Richardson and John Osborne which are worthy of Edmund Kean and might indeed have been written about him. I gather that the photography is superbly stark, and that it moves fast despite its wordiness. We shall see. I go full out and have I hope extracted every ounce of comedy. It contains one forgets a great deal of mad savage humour. People's reactions are very illuminating. They don't say the usual "great" "fabulous" "wonderful". They in fact say hardly anything at all. They appear to be stunned and can't really discuss it for several hours and then the praise is lavish. What is curious is that they all seem to be profoundly moved and are all desperately sorry and sympathetic for Jimmy Porter. Two hard-boiled ladies who saw it were so compelled by Porter that they started to take an active dislike to Mary Ure. I hope that that is not general. And I promise you that there isn't a shred of self-pity in my performance. I am for the first time ever looking forward to seeing a film in which I play.

Much of my time in late 1959 was taken up in preparing the groundwork with others, notably Shepard Traube, for the formation of the Society of Stage Directors and Choreographers

(SSDC). We desperately needed to establish our rights and have them protected. The first annual meeting took place on 24 November. Later I became the Executive Vice-President of the Society. I was kept busy with a Shakespeare class and with a rewrite in collaboration with two experienced authors, Lou Solomon and Henry Myers, of a new play which I was to direct. I signed a contract but the producer reneged on it, an exemplary proof of the necessity for the SSDC. But I had enjoyed working with the two playwrights.

On 28 November Richard, still in Hollywood, phoned me to say that Sybil in Switzerland had given birth the day before to a second daughter, Jessica. Speaking to him, Sybil had been wonderful in reconciling him to being so far away. In less than a week he was on his way home and we had two good meetings. Later he sent me a welcome cheque as a Christmas gift.

I thoroughly enjoyed preparing and delivering a lecture to the Bernard Shaw Society entitled 'Shaw on Shakespeare'. As I prepared it I thought of how I first became aware of Bernard Shaw, a reminiscence I had shared with Richard, probably more than once. It's a remarkable example of Shaw's dramatic method, and was told to me when I was a boy beginning to be intellectually curious. During the Boer War a protest meeting was held in the Workmen's Hall in Mountain Ash, my birthplace. The coal miners had built the Hall which, in addition to meeting rooms, a library, a gymnasium and a swimming pool, had quite an impressive theatre. It was probably in 1900 that the meeting took place. The three speakers were Keir Hardie, the first Socialist Member of Parliament, the 'Vicar of Radstock', the first avowed Socialist clergyman of the Church of England, and Bernard Shaw. They spoke in that order. As Shaw, with his famous beard and breeches, advanced to the footlights, the audience eagerly anticipated some examples of his renowned wit, but his opening words stunned them into incredulous silence: 'I believe in war.' He went on to say, 'Because I'm too old to fight and I can make money out of it.' In his plays he uses the stage as a pulpit, but shocks people into thinking for themselves by apparently giving the best arguments to those he doesn't himself agree with, such as Undershaft, the armaments manufacturer in *Major Barbara*.

Richard was in New York for most of January 1960, chiefly to do a good television play with Maximilian Schell, *The Fifth Column*. I had some enjoyable meetings with him, but they occurred with exasperating unreliability; several times he broke appointments with me but made up for them with surprise appearances and explanations which soon won me over. In that same month I also had some interesting meetings with Maximilian; we had become good friends during our work together on *Interlock*. In my diary I wrote of him, 'He has everything to succeed, including an exemplary singleness of purpose; he has even turned down the lead in what promises to be a good musical.' There was moreover a special purpose in our meetings at that time; he wanted to study *Hamlet* with me. He knew the Schlegel translation as well as I knew the original. Many Germans feel sorry for us that we don't know Schlegel because his nineteenth-century German is so much easier to understand than Shakespeare's English. My work with Max was to bear surprising fruit in 1962, when he invited me to help cast and rehearse actors for a dubbed version of the highly successful German film of *Hamlet*, in which he had starred.

Since not one of the several projects I was presently involved in was coming to a head, I decided to take a break by going to Europe, and did so for six weeks, travelling this time by air. A cable from Sybil led me to book a further flight from London to Geneva for my first visit to Villa Le Pays de Galles. Richard met me in Geneva. The Scofields, Paul and Joy, were staying with them. The three of us were very comfortable in the guest house in the lovely grounds. It was wonderful to be remembered by Kate, and to see for the first time the beautiful new baby, Jessica. The weather was fine but the farmers were crying out for rain; there had not been a drop in two months. We made several excursions to first-class restaurants that justified their reputations, and I had some interesting talks with Paul Scofield, whom I got to know as I had not before. There were also shopping expeditions to Nyon, beautiful walks, and trips on the lake in

Richard's boat. In spite of all the social activities, Richard saw to it that we had some very good talks *à deux*.

To my own surprise, on my return journey I stayed a whole happy month in Britain, half in London and half in Wales. I had such a good time that again I hesitated about leaving. I even wrote to both Richard and the Baruths to tell them about my renewed dilemma. In the letter to Richard I described how I had made a tour of the Vale of Glamorgan to find the most desirable place to live and had decided on Llantwit Major. In his reply he said that, if I really meant it, he would buy me a house there. But I had found that I didn't really mean it. So I returned to New York, where Richard and the family were soon to join me. He had been offered the part of King Arthur in a new musical, *Camelot*; at the time I had no idea what that was going to mean for me. They asked me to find an apartment for them, and I did so in the Beresford on Central Park West. I was happy about the location because it was within easy walking distance not only of my apartment but also that of Aaron Frosch and his wife and three young daughters. For several years Aaron had been Richard's lawyer, and for me he was my Rock of Gibraltar. I visited his home almost every week and looked forward to our Sunday walks in Central Park with the three children; soon Kate would be able to join us. I phoned Sybil in Switzerland about the accommodation. Madge, the woman who cleaned for me, agreed to take on the much bigger job of the Burton apartment at the Beresford, and she had only a short while to get it ready. Richard arrived six days before Sybil and the children, and spent most of that time with me.

As soon as Richard got hold of the script and score of *Camelot* we set to work on his three big solos and a duet. There was a piano in the apartment. In my youth I had taught myself to play and was a fairly good sight reader, but I think this was the only time I had played the piano in America. I didn't miss it because I wasn't good enough to satisfy myself. My mind flashed back to the time when, at Richard's insistent request, I had taught him finger by finger to play the first movement of Beethoven's Moonlight Sonata, and he had become sufficiently adept at it to surprise people when the show-off mood was on him. After our initial work on the *Camelot* numbers, the company's rehearsal pianist took over. I had some pleasant sessions with Richard in which we went over his lines, and I felt the show had potential.

Richard met the family at Idlewild while I waited in the apartment, 15G. Sybil and three-year-old Kate were in fine form but Jessica had not stood the journey well; she soon recovered, however. A typical entry in my diary at this time reads:

> *Thursday, September 1st.* Kate came to stay with me while her mother went to a *Camelot* reading. She was no trouble and adhered to her schedule, including the nap after 'dindins'. I took her to the park. It was fascinating to watch her reaction to the other children in the playground, particularly in the sand-pit. She was very eager to make contact, and finally did with a charming little girl called 'Alex'; but she had some rebuffs. She was even happy fetching and carrying for a little boy.

On 12 September I attended the first run-through of Act 1 of *Camelot*. In my diary I wrote: 'Never has Richard's overwhelming stage-magic been more apparent.' The following month I went to see a performance of the musical in Toronto, where it was the first production in the vast new O'Keefe Center, which by its very size and newness was bound to have serious acoustic problems. I found the theatre impressive in itself but theatrically forbidding. Worse still, the show was in real trouble and needed major constructional surgery. Apart from anything else, it was four and a half hours long. My diary records what happened next:

> *Friday, October 7th.* A memorable day. I spent some six hours making notes on the script and last night's performance. In the afternoon I gave a long series of detailed notes to R., and in the evening a near-miracle happened; he gave an inspired performance which galvanized the whole cast; he took advantage of every one of my notes and brought them all off superbly. Afterwards we went to a very dull party until 3 a.m.

Sybil and Kate arrived the next day, having left Jessica in New York with her nurse, Marta. That afternoon I went to the matineé. It is usual for the next performance after a successful opening to be a let-down, but this one wasn't. The following day, Sunday, Richard and Sybil had to go to a party for the cast. Roddy McDowell, who was playing Mordred, chose not to go; instead he came to see me, and we discussed his part for several hours. I found him to be an unusually sensitive, intelligent actor.

Sybil and Kate were in Toronto for only three days. I took Kate for a couple of happy excursions, one of which was to Center Island on the ferry. When we returned to the mainland we couldn't find a taxi, and she was so tired that I had to carry her all the way home.

The day after Sybil and Kate left I did too, but to visit my Cleveland friends, the Thomases. While I was in Cleveland I was surprised by a phone call from Sybil to say that Moss Hart, the director of *Camelot*, had had a heart attack. (He didn't return to the show, and a year after its Broadway opening he died.) Just prior to the director's forced withdrawal from the production, Alan Jay Lerner, the author and lyricist, had himself been ill and in hospital. It seemed as if the show were doomed. In addition to the tremendous task of cutting and revising the text, Lerner now had the added one of directing the emended version.

After five pleasant days in Cleveland I returned by train to New York, which now meant primarily Sybil and Kate. We were successful in finding a school for Kate just across the Park. She enjoyed her first day there so much that she cried when it was time to go home.

Camelot moved to Boston. The theatre world was full of wild rumours about its imminent closure. Sybil went to Boston for a few days during which I spent much of my time with Kate and Jessica. She phoned to say that the show was still in great trouble, but the audience reaction was better than in Toronto. At Richard's invitation I went to Boston the following week and was with him for his thirty-fifth birthday, which was celebrated by a party on stage after the performance. During the party Alan

Jay Lerner asked me to have breakfast with him in the morning; it was later postponed to lunch.

I had heard that, since the departure of Moss Hart, Richard had shared my extensive notes on the script with the author, and it was my dream that I might be asked in to help. The dream had been encouraged by Sybil, who had heard things to this effect, so I was not unduly surprised after the luncheon conversation to be asked to take over the direction of the show. We went together to the theatre for the rehearsal of some new material which involved Richard, but he could not be found. There was an immediate crisis but I kept calm because I guessed the reason for his disappearance: he was in a turmoil because of his concern for me – he desperately wanted me to take over the show both for his sake and mine. The rehearsal was cancelled. Instead, Alan and I had a long and late session, the first of many.

I readily agreed to the terms for my engagement. I was to be adequately paid, but Moss Hart, quite rightly, was to retain the billing as director; I was to receive no billing. The following day I began three weeks of work, the most strenuous I can remember. I saw all performances and gave notes after every one, rehearsed the Equity-allowed five hours a day (less on matinée days), and had sessions with Alan Jay Lerner that lasted until the early hours of the morning. Rarely did I get more than four hours' sleep. I had an excellent rapport with the company and with the choreographer, Hanya Holm. I thoroughly enjoyed the hectic schedule. With large cuts, new scenes and new numbers, and even a new set, it was a great strain on the company to play one version by night and rehearse another by day until gradually, scene by scene, the new material was incorporated into the show the public saw. I should have liked at least a further week of rehearsal, but the glamorous Broadway opening took place on Saturday 3 December in the Majestic Theatre. The special opening-night programme had a note of appreciation for my contribution to the production. There was, however, a somewhat regrettable postscript; it didn't upset me at all, but it did Richard.

In 1978 Alan Jay Lerner's autobiography, *The Street where I*

Lived, appeared, and in it he makes no mention of my work on *Camelot*. He gives the impression that he alone took over the direction of the show after Moss Hart had to leave. The following year he approached Richard about a twentieth-anniversary revival of the musical. In a letter written to me from Hollywood on 4 November 1979 Richard says, 'I gave Alan Jay Lerner 5 minutes of ice-cold hell for not mentioning in his autobiography that it was *you* who saved the show. I'll make up for it in one of my pieces one of these days.' He didn't live to write that piece.

I received much heart-warming appreciation from members of the company; they knew what I had done. A treasured memento of the first night is a gift from a member of the chorus. (She was an excellent photographer. Most young actors, singers and dancers on Broadway have to have a second profession from which to make a living until the next engagement.) It is an album of very good photographs taken without my knowledge at rehearsals I conducted; it's a perfect reminder of an exciting chapter in my life.

CHAPTER
Eight

Every director feels somewhat bereft when his production opens; he misses the stimulation of the work and the daily fellowship of the company. This time, however, I had the compensation of having the family at hand, including Graham, Richard's younger brother. Professionally, by early 1961 I had resumed my life of waiting for possibilities to mature. A new would-be producer, William Chambers, brought to my attention a play called *Udomo*, derived from the novel *A Wreath for Udomo*, which itself had obviously been suggested by the remarkable career of Nkrumah, the founder of the Republic of Ghana. The trouble was that the novel was much better written than the play; even so, after a few sessions with the playwright, William Branch, I signed a contract to direct *Udomo*. My relations with Branch were difficult; I suppose I was too critical and so, naturally, he became defensive. It was hoped that Sidney Poitier would play the lead, but his film commitments prevented that. Brock Peters was the next choice, and a very good one, but later this safe casting was called into question by an exciting reading by Bernie Hamilton. When I discussed the matter with Richard he said, 'Go for the exciting one, even if you have to fire him in Boston.'

Richard had recently provided the brilliant and sensitive narration for a television series about Winston Churchill. At that time I was also working with him and Cathleen Nesbit on a poetry recital to be given on a Thursday afternoon in the Theatre de Lys; I was to do the introductions. Richard was particularly memorable in an extract he had made his own from that great book by David Jones, *In Parenthesis*. It's a soliloquy by Dai, a Welsh soldier in France in World War I, expressing his kinship with soldiers throughout the ages, even those at the foot of the Cross.

Much of my time was taken up with auditions for *Udomo*, and I gave a presentation of the play in a large room in a Fifth Avenue apartment which was jam-packed with potential backers. We even staged readings in the hope of raising money.

An amusing incident occurred in March. At short notice Richard and Sybil were giving a very private after-show party in their apartment in honour of two couples: Sir Laurence Olivier and Joan Plowright, to celebrate their wedding that day, and Jason Robards and his lady friend, to celebrate Jason's divorce. Sybil asked for my help; in particular, could I get hold of a wedding cake? I went to several places without success, but finally located a magnificent unclaimed birthday cake. The confectioner covered the inappropriate inscription with a splendid decoration depicting a bridal couple. I warned Sybil to cut around the wedding decoration, but one of the guests – I think it was the new Lady Olivier – was so enamoured of it that she took it off the cake as a souvenir of the occasion, revealing the words Happy Birthday.

I went to Harlem to make another presentation of *Udomo* in the continuing quest to raise money, and the reception was so enthusiastic that again I was given false hopes of a production. William Chambers now advised me not to turn down any other offer of work, and so, when Arnold Moss asked me to direct him as Malvolio in a small-scale production of *Twelfth Night* in Washington, DC, I agreed after some slight hesitation. The rehearsals went well, and the school matinée was a particular joy; the production deserved far more performances than the three or four free ones. I came back to make still more fund-raising appearances for *Udomo*, for which I was getting an occasional advance on my director's fee.

Richard brought me a project that a producer had suggested to him. It was to write a screenplay from Dylan Thomas's *The*

Beach of Falesá. The name of Dylan Thomas spelt magic to both Richard and me, and I eagerly set to work. Dylan had visualized the story as a screenplay but it still required much work. When the book was published it was stated in the publicity that Richard was about to make a film of it, but he never did, though he and I shared meetings with Israel Berman, the potential producer. Meanwhile *Camelot* continued its successful run, enabling me to spend every Sunday with the family. Here is a typical entry in my diary:

> *Sunday, July 16th.* The usual trip with Kate to the Park; she had 9 rides on the carousel. When we got back, Paul and Joy Scofield had arrived from Canada. A most enjoyable evening ensued. All five of us went to the Plaza Oak Room for an excellent dinner. Then R. had the brainwave that we should go home through the Park in a horse-carriage. I've long wanted to do that but never had the nerve for it. On a summer evening it truly is delightful.

Cis and Elfed came over for a visit in August, and I spent some time alone with them. I remember taking them on the boat trip around Manhattan. Elfed looked better than ever he had since I had known him – he was obviously enjoying his comfortable retirement – and Cis was and is a never-ceasing joy. On one of my periodic visits to *Camelot* I noted, 'R. has experimented like mad, but I don't approve of all the results.'

When I had virtually given up hope of achieving a production of *Udomo*, a plan developed to do it in London. At the same time I was approached by Noel Behn, to whom I owed *Purple Dust*, to head a New York school of musical theatre, which he was thinking of starting on a commercial basis. His argument for it was fundamentally sound: the musical is the most distinctively American contribution to theatre, and yet there was no place where a would-be professional performer could be well trained in the three necessary departments of acting, singing and dancing. With *Udomo* in prospect, I could not commit myself. Douglas Crawford, who was behind the proposed London production, urged me not only to direct that play there, but to stay to do other shows, including a musical he was planning for Ian Carmichael. The Lyric Theatre, Hammersmith, had been offered to us for three weeks. After discussing it with me, William Chambers and Douglas Crawford decided to accept the offer; if the production was the success they hoped for, it could be transferred to the West End. For me the Lyric, Hammersmith, was cherished ground: it was there that Richard had scored two memorable successes in his early career, *The Boy with the Cart* and *Montserrat*. Tony Walton, a brilliant stage designer and at that time the husband of Julie Andrews, was engaged for *Udomo*, and we had some long and stimulating discussions about it. William Chambers was enthusiastic about Tony's ideas, and I became excited by the physical possibilities of the production.

Sunday 17 September was a Farewell day. On the Friday I had seen Richard in *Camelot* for what I assumed would be the last time; he gave a superb performance. I was leaving for London on the Tuesday. Sybil with her usual efficiency was packing for their imminent departure for Switzerland; Richard was leaving *Camelot* to make the film of *Cleopatra* in Rome. In spite of all the farewells that Sunday, I managed to have my hour in the Park with Kate.

When I arrived in London I was warmly welcomed by Ivor and Gwen, with whom I was to stay. Their home was a haven of comfort during what proved to be the most difficult event in my professional career. After three weeks they left to join Richard and Sybil in Rome, but I stayed in their home for another seven weeks, the first two of which were spent casting. The production was in financial trouble from the start, and in the second week I was told by William Chambers that the cast had to be reduced from thirty-five to twenty-five. There were several 'crowd' scenes, and this impoverishment entailed some drastic rethinking.

We had three weeks to rehearse a complicated production. The great majority of the cast, including the leads, were black. Some of them embodied strange mixtures; thus, one actor was very Cockney in speech but had been born in Port Talbot of an African father and a Welsh mother. Certain actors sometimes annoyed me by their unpunctuality and lack of application. The physical production, the work of Tony Walton, was remarkable, and included some set projections; however, it was too complicated for the stage staff and crew to master in the limited time we had for technical rehearsals, and so it followed that our most faultless show was our last. And there were personal conflicts, particularly between the producer and the author. Twice the producer had to fly back to New York to try to raise more money; he still owed us money when we closed. To add to the complications, I myself had a bad attack of food poisoning during rehearsals.

The central figure in the final disaster was Edric Connor, who played the part of Mhendi. He and his wife, Pearl, were popular leaders of the black community in London, and they had been very helpful in the initial stages of the production. Let my diary tell the sad story:

Wednesday, November 1st. What a day! Bits-and-pieces and run-through in the afternoon, followed by an extraordinary evening: a charity performance, organized by Pearl Connor, to establish Negro Theatre in London. It was a preview. The audience, largely black and distinguished, reacted wildly to the politics and sex in the play. The technical side was way off, so I insisted on a complete technical run-through after the show; I hope it did some good.

Thursday, November 2nd. The never-to-be-forgotten first-night. Edric Connor had been reluctant to go on; he obviously has some psychosomatic reaction to first-night nerves. He ruined the show by his first scene and completely collapsed on stage at the opening of the second act. I had to make a curtain speech, closing the show. What a shambles afterwards, with the press crawling everywhere! This should be the biggest professional disaster of my life, but I'm calm – or numb.

Friday, November 3rd. Management has decided to fire Connor and replace him with Leo Carera. Branch has at last agreed to drastic cutting of the script. There was a dreadful scene in the theatre in the morning. Connor turned up although he had been fired. I hid in corners, pubs, and cafés, working with Carera. Connor is fighting Chambers over the dismissal, and he seems to have the press entirely on his side. I took Carera home with me and we worked late into the night.

Saturday, November 4th. I called a rehearsal of the Mhendi scenes. Again Connor and the press turned up. I find the embarrassing situation hard to take, but I managed to get in a good rehearsal. The cuts are a great improvement. I sense that the principals in the company are solidly anti-Connor, but the press isn't.

Sunday, November 5th. A rehearsal in Bill Chambers' apartment; tiring and unsatisfactory. Carera is not a quick study and this worries me a bit. Hobson and T.C. Worsley [two leading critics] have had the gall to review *Udomo* on the basis of that dreadful, unfinished first-night. I feel fairly certain that the play has had it now, especially since the popular press is espousing Connor's case against the management. Poor Bill Chambers!

Monday, November 6th. A good rehearsal in the afternoon but am worried that Carera is an incredibly slow study; it's hard for me to hide my exasperation. Earl Cameron [who played Udomo] too is very slow in absorbing cuts and changes; perhaps it's because they don't get enough theatre work. I was appalled to find that there was an audience for the dress-rehearsal at night; it was most unfair to Carera, but the show went quite well.

Tuesday, November 7th. Words are still a problem for Carera, but he's a good actor. The preview at night went quite well, even technically, but I'm afraid that success leading to a transfer calls for a miracle now.

Wednesday, November 8th. Worked with Carera up to almost the last minute. He seems intelligent and yet some of his paraphrases are stupid. For our second first-night the house was far from full. The show went quite well, and Carera came through better than I had feared.

Thursday, November 9th. The notices are universally bad for the play, but there are a few quite good ones for the production. The question now is whether the show can even fulfil the Hammersmith engagement. Another question is whether Bill Chambers can pay what he owes. I am curiously calm about it all.

Friday, November 10th. The play comes off tomorrow. Poor Bill Chambers is the only one I think of in the mess.

Saturday, November 11th. Bill Chambers has gone to America without leaving money for the cast, but I'm sure he's gone to raise money. The last show was good; it really deserves a chance to find its audience.

Richard was so concerned about the effect the *Udomo* experience might have had on me that he urged me to join the family, but I decided to stay in London another two weeks to see my many friends. I didn't go to Wales because my Mountain Ash family, Megan and Fred Blackmore, had come to London to see the last night of *Udomo*, which was the best performance.

I finally left for Rome on 28 November. Richard and Ivor met me, and my diary records 'a wonderful welcome in a wonderful house'. On my first day there were several notable visitors: Rex Harrison and Rachel Roberts, Hume Cronin and Jessica Tandy, and Ricardo Montalban, who proved to be a great raconteur. The Cronins generously gave a dinner party for me on my fifty-seventh birthday, which fell soon after my arrival. Of course, I saw a great deal of Kate and I particularly remember going with her and her father to the zoo. I also read the script of *Cleopatra*, and thought it better than I had expected; visiting the Cinecittà Studios, I found the sets for the film to be unbelievably impressive in size, lavishness and attention to detail. Richard left for New York to take part in a Lerner–Lowe television show, and Sybil flew out to join him four days later, just for the weekend, but their return was delayed for two days. In their absence I spent much of my time sightseeing, often accompanied by Ivor and Gwen. We explored an underground tomb on the Appian Way, saw the thrilling S. Clemente Church, the huge baths of Caracalla, the morbidly impressive Resistance cemetery at Ardiante, and the tawdry Quo Vadis Church. I also did my best to console Kate, who missed her mother very much.

The high point of my visit to Rome was yet to come. After Richard returned, he drove Ivor and me to Naples, chiefly to see Pompeii. There I climbed to the topmost row of the ancient amphitheatre, which had been built to hold thousands. Richard stood far below on the stage, and we repeated our old Port Talbot mountain exercise; the acoustics were breathtakingly perfect. What did they know 2,000 years ago that our acousticians don't seem to know today?

The next day, 18 December, I returned to London. I was determined to spend Christmas in Wales. Later it struck me forcibly that, while in Rome, I had met many of those associated with the making of *Cleopatra*, including the producer, Walter Wanger, and the director, Joseph Mankiewicz, but I had not met Cleopatra herself, Elizabeth Taylor.

Christmas in Mountain Ash didn't disappoint me; it never did. I stayed with my niece and her family for ten days. She is the daughter of my half-brother, Will Wilson, who was eighteen years my senior; he was always a joy to be with. While in Mountain Ash I made a brief visit to Port Talbot. I flew back to America first-class, Richard having given me a spare ticket. It was the first time I had ever done so, and I thought it quite luxurious. I was returning to start work on the film script of *The Beach of Falesá*, which Richard had requested me to write. However, my first professional activity was to visit Noel Behn's Musical Theatre Academy. It was on 23rd Street in a commodious old nineteenth-century building, which has since disappeared. The three departments were headed by distinguished professionals: Sanford Meisner (acting), Lehman Engel (singing) and Hanya Holm (dancing).

As soon as I could contact Bill Chambers I took him to lunch and was relieved to find that he seemed to have survived the *Udomo* disaster well. For my part, I was in a bad way for a week or so with inflamed neck muscles, but I made myself go to see Paul Scofield in *A Man for All Seasons*; he was very impressive.

We had a good meeting after the show, and he came to lunch the following day. The better I knew him the more I liked him. He was an actor dedicated to theatre, whereas Richard had strayed into show business.

When I was able to resume my usual activities, I went to see *Camelot*, which was still in good shape. Afterwards, I went backstage and received my usual warm welcome. It happened that Gladys Cooper was in the audience and also came backstage. The coincidence resulted in another very pleasant meeting; a major topic of conversation now was the Hardys, Robert and Sally. Gradually I settled down to work on *The Beach of Falesá*, but there was no urgency to spur me on until I agreed to direct a production of Chekhov's *Three Sisters* in Brooklyn College; that prompted me to work seriously on *Falesá* before rehearsals absorbed my time and energy.

Since my return, Richard and Kate had spoken to me once from Rome, but I was totally unprepared for what happened on Friday 16 February. At 7 a.m. I was awakened by a call from a very distraught Sybil. She had left Richard because of his involvement with Elizabeth Taylor! She was staying in Roddy McDowell's vacant apartment on Central Park West. I went up to her at once and, after talking to her, decided to send a cable to Richard in Rome. That prompted an angry call from him; apparently I had been 'very indiscreet'; it seemed that the paparazzi had got hold of the contents of my cable. Richard's anger was met by mine. As soon as we hung up I wrote him a very strong letter, but I didn't speak to him again for two years.

CHAPTER
Nine

I cancelled my engagements in order to be with Sybil, who had now calmed down. On two successive evenings I was able to take her out to dinner, and we even went to a Marx Brothers movie. I became optimistic that all would yet be well, but the following day Richard phoned Sybil; he was in the worst possible mood, and her distress was renewed. The children were still in Rome and he wanted her to take them to Switzerland, but she insisted on taking them to London instead. She left that very day for Rome, and I took her to the Idlewild Airport. My optimism faded.

Rumours began to abound, and the press kept my phone busy. I received some calls from friends in London because of a false report that I was seriously ill. As soon as Sybil left I set to work on *Three Sisters*, but work on *Falesá* was impossible. No word came from Richard or Sybil, and my anxiety increased.

It was two weeks before I had a letter from Rome. It was from Sybil, and I gathered that she was having a very difficult time. She told me that Richard had been infuriated by my letter. I decided it was best for me to keep busy, so in addition to the *Three Sisters* production I took on two classes, one at the Musical Theatre Academy and a private one. I even forced myself to do some work on *Falesá*, probably out of remorse for my unrelenting attitude to Richard, and I agreed with Arnold Moss to direct another Shakespeare production in Washington, DC; this time it was *Macbeth*. Noel Behn tried to persuade me to become the Director of the Musical Theatre Academy; my initial response was a strong no, but it gradually weakened in two months to a dubious yes.

In the middle of rehearsals of *Three Sisters* a most unexpected thing happened. A growth appeared on my tongue, and I began to have difficulty in swallowing. I was so busy that I put off going to my doctor. When I finally did go, he arranged an immediate appointment for me with a specialist. After that gentleman had looked at the growth he left the room and returned with two associates, and I heard comments that suggested they had discovered a rare gem. 'Have you ever seen a better one? We must show it at the meeting next week.' A camera clicked, and then a bit of the growth was taken for a biopsy. My state of mind can be imagined, but I managed to ask, 'Is it cancer?' My question was dismissed with, 'Cancer's a word.' Then I was told that I should go to the hospital the following morning to commence treatment leading to an operation in two weeks' time. His final comment I can still hear: 'I'll save as much of your tongue as possible.' The psychosomatic effect of this experience was such that by evening I had lost my voice, and I had to cancel all engagements; I could barely speak on the phone. I shared my news with a few close friends, and wrote to Mountain Ash and Rome. I had told Aaron Frosch, and apparently he phoned Richard, who said categorically that on no account was I to be robbed of my tongue; I suppose he thought I'd rather be dead. The following morning, just as I was leaving to be taken to the hospital by Al Baruth, the phone rang. Al answered it. It was the specialist cancelling the hospital appointment and asking me to go to see him instead. I did so. The biopsy had proved to be completely negative. The doctor's comment was, 'I'll never trust my eyes again.' He put me on antibiotics and I resumed my full schedule the following day, having sent happy cables to Mountain Ash and Rome. In less than a week all the trouble had disappeared.

Aaron had kept in touch with developments in Rome, and from him I learned that Sybil and the children had moved to London; no resolution of the situation was in sight. The brouhaha was increased by the presence in New York of Eddie Fisher, the husband of Elizabeth Taylor. Although he was in hospital he gave interviews to the press. They were after me too, but I managed to evade them. Every day there were pictures of Richard and Elizabeth together. I was much cheered by a letter from Sybil, determined to save the marriage, but on the same day I was disturbed to read that Elizabeth and Eddie Fisher were about to get divorced. I was rarely at home, but occasionally a reporter would catch me; I resolutely refused comment. I remember one persistent man from the *Post*, who told me he would lose his job if I didn't co-operate with him on a series about Richard; I refused but felt a little uncomfortable. I was embarrassed at that time to receive from Richard, through Aaron, a cheque for $650 to pay off the income tax I owed. I feel sure that Aaron prompted it. I didn't need it, and certainly didn't want it under the circumstances; it was Richard's way of maintaining contact, and I appreciated it as such. Then, two days later, headlines shouted that Richard and Sybil were spending the weekend together in Paris. They did meet there, but failed to come to an agreement. Richard had gone in answer to a direct appeal from Sybil.

No sooner had *Three Sisters* opened successfully in Brooklyn than I was in rehearsal with *Macbeth*. Arnold Moss had collected a good cast. On Good Friday a long letter came from Emlyn Williams, who had gone to Rome to make a direct appeal to Richard on behalf of Sybil and the children. I'm sure a part of Richard must have been moved by this, but the strongly independent part of him would have resented it as an interference in his private life. I myself admired Emlyn for his initiative, and was very grateful to him for his concern. But on Easter Sunday I received bad news: Richard was asking Sybil for a divorce. I just could not believe it.

For some time Sanford Meisner had been pressing me to accept Noel Behn's invitation to become the Director of the Musical Theatre Academy, but I continued to be reluctant to do so, especially when I heard that it was in dire need of money. However, Noel Behn was relentless in his pursuit of me. In my diary I commented, 'It looks as if I'm being dragged into the orbit of the Academy willy-nilly, but I must preserve my freedom somehow.' Meanwhile I continued fitful work on *The Beach of Falesá*, though I now had little hope of its coming to fruition. I suppose I did it because it gave me some imaginative contact with Richard. After observing every teacher in the Academy at work and being very impressed, though I sensed discontent and machinations, and after meeting with the students and finding them truly enthusiastic, I finally decided to become the Director; I started my duties on 28 May 1962.

Then three days later I got a call from Israel Berman, who was hoping to produce *The Beach of Falesá*. He had been to Rome to see Richard (there were still three months of filming to do on *Cleopatra*) and brought me warm greetings from him. This did not induce me to write to Richard, because I could not accept the situation, but it did cause me to press on with the *Falesá* script, which I delivered less than a month later to Israel Berman, together with my film script of *Coriolanus*, about which he had heard from Richard.

At this time I was also intensely occupied with the Society of Stage Directors and Choreographers; we were having our first, difficult negotiations with the League of New York Theatres, and I was one of the negotiators. This kind of work is very necessary but I don't enjoy it. Ironically I was by way of being on the opposite side at the Academy, where I was having to persuade the staff to accept cuts in salary. I was saddened but not at all resentful when some left rather than agree to this.

Emlyn Williams came to New York in July – he had to replace Paul Scofield in *A Man for All Seasons* – and I had some good and reassuring meetings with him. He hadn't given up hope of a reconciliation between Richard and Sybil, and he gave me a comforting report of a weekend Sybil had spent with Molly, his wife. By disappointing contrast, a meeting at this time with Israel Berman revealed that we were completely opposed in our attitudes to *The Beach of Falesá*; this was the end of the project for me. We had a further session later in the summer, and a very pleasant dinner together, but without a meeting of minds.

In August I heard from Aaron that Richard and Sybil were

together again in Celigny. It was a wonderful surprise and my heart bounded with hope. I wrote to them jointly at once. But Emlyn Williams advised me not to be too optimistic; he did not think that Elizabeth Taylor was out of the picture. I didn't hear from Celigny but sent a present there for Kate's fifth birthday.

It had become increasingly clear to me that, if we were to maintain its high standards, we could not continue to run the Musical Theatre Academy as a commercial venture. With the new term beginning in less than a week, there was near chaos in the Academy office, which meant some very late nights for me. By the time school opened I was beyond sleep and so a little crotchety, but all went smoothly. I had arranged to do some teaching at the Academy, and this I enjoyed. I taught Rhetoric and Verse-speaking to the senior students. I also gave a public Shakespeare class, the proceeds of which I shared with the Academy. Meanwhile, my work with the Society of Stage Directors and Choreographers continued. At a meeting of the Legal Committee in early October the bye-laws were changed to give extra power to the Executive Vice-President. This was very flattering because it was assumed that I would be elected to that office, as indeed I was three weeks later.

About two months had passed since I had had any news from Celigny, but at last, in early October, came a letter from Sybil. I opened it eagerly but it was very distressing; there was really no change in the situation. I felt unable to act for fear of making things worse. My next letter from Sybil was very different from the previous one, though again nothing had changed. Her strength of character and purpose was remarkable, so much so that I became optimistic once more. I wrote to her and Kate in that spirit, but when Richard's birthday came round on 10 November I ignored it, although I felt guilty about doing so.

In mid-December Sybil wrote again, asking me to phone her. When I did so she sounded very self-possessed, but she had been going through hell, having virtually decided to force Richard to choose between her and Elizabeth. She expected me to confirm her decision but I advised caution; Richard was not a man to challenge but to persuade. I was so worried about the situation that I couldn't sleep, yet I had to put on a happy face for the Christmas party at the Academy. I gave a reading of Dylan Thomas's *A Child's Christmas in Wales*, which was to become an annual event.

I was ill for a time after Christmas and had to stay at home. My recovery wasn't helped by a phone call from a friend who had read in the Philadelphia papers that Richard and Sybil were getting divorced. I wouldn't believe it because I didn't want to. Once back in harness I had a lot of work to make up, and I welcomed it. Primarily I had to plan the timetable for the fast-approaching new term at the Academy, and that involved not only the class schedules but private singing lessons for each student. I even took on some more commitments, such as a lecture at Smith College and a programme at the Poetry Center with Edward Mulhare and Nancy Wickwire; it was called *A Late Valentine*.

My diary records that in the first months of 1963 I was often irritable and unsociable. I suppose it must have been the fear of losing Richard, because I felt that if Sybil lost him I would too. The first of March that year was the twentieth anniversary of his fully coming into my life. It was a sad day because we did not exchange greetings. Then at the end of March it was confirmed by Aaron's office that Richard and Sybil had decided on a divorce. Aaron went to Europe to arrange it, and Sybil and the children came back with him to New York. Her strength of mind did much to reconcile me to her decision.

Journalistic hell broke loose, so much so that I couldn't stay in my apartment; it was besieged. The office telephone was kept busy, lots of the calls being from London, but I didn't have to deal with those; Mr Burton wasn't available. Sybil remained hidden away in a hotel. I took the children out to Central Park almost stealthily, but on one occasion a press photographer spotted us and followed us to the hotel. When the picture appeared in the newspaper, the caption described me as 'an unidentified man'. Sybil had to change her hotel, and did so by night. I was very cutting to people who questioned me. I continued my expeditions to the Park with Kate and Jessica but, whenever possible, we joined up with Aaron's three children.

At this time I was negotiating to buy a house, the first I had ever owned. It was on West 22nd Street and had been used as a convent for many years, but the nuns were leaving it for a new one. It was a large nineteenth-century house with five storeys and a cellar; the main room on the second floor had been made into a chapel with stained-glass windows. My plan was to turn the two top floors into a self-contained apartment, the income from which would be most welcome. I had been encouraged in the purchase by a protégé of mine, Richard Alderson, known professionally as Christian Alderson, but I wouldn't have gone ahead with the plan without Aaron's full approval. Christian had come to my notice in a way that was characteristic of him.

In 1962 Noel Behn had run a summer school to raise money for the Academy. Apart from the organization I had little to do with it, being solely concerned with the full-time students. Far more females than males enrolled, and Noel had the bright idea of giving free admission to a number of young male professionals who wanted further training. One of those chosen was Christian Alderson, who was at that time a dancer in *My Fair Lady* on Broadway. At the end of the summer school my secretary told me that one of the students wanted to see me. It was Christian. He wanted to thank me for the course (he was the only one to do so) but, much more than that, he wanted to express his gratitude by doing something for the school. He had been down to the basement and thought he could turn it into a little theatre. In his spare time he worked for months without charging the school a penny, and provided us with a good stage, seating for about a hundred and, at the back of the auditorium, three voice studios. The Academy was greatly enriched by Christian's work, and to show my gratitude I took him out to dinner a few times. I soon discovered he had great natural talent and was eager to learn. Was this to be a repetition of the Richard experience? Very soon he was giving outstanding performances in some of my productions, and I foresaw a starry future for him, but then he underwent a profound and enduring spiritual refocusing of his life, and completely abandoned his theatrical ambitions. He became a very devout, but not at all pietistic, Roman Catholic, and has since had a greater influence on me than I on him. Christian has an acute aesthetic sensitivity, and he it was who turned the convent into a beautiful home. He also found for me my present house in Key West and devoted two years to making it perfect for my retirement.

Easter 1963 was a very happy time for me because of the presence of Sybil and the children. Looking after the girls was the best way to keep thoughts and conversation off Richard. On the Monday Sybil came to lunch in my apartment and was waylaid in the lobby by a reporter who had been hanging around there for weeks, but she had become used to such encounters and it didn't upset her unduly. After lunch we went down to see the house I was in the process of acquiring; she seemed to be genuinely thrilled by it.

The Academy's financial troubles had now reached a crisis, and I called a staff meeting to announce that there was no money in our bank account. It was a surprisingly uplifting experience – a spirit of camaraderie had been engendered, and the teachers were determined that the Academy should not be closed. One of them even offered a goodly portion of her life's savings to help. The same spirit seemed to infect the student body, resulting in a particularly good Showcase, the performance given by students completing the two-year course. It was chiefly intended for possible employers and agents and took place in an off-Broadway theatre, the Van Damm. In the audience was a group of Russians who were representing their film industry in the negotiations for a film based on Mitchell Wilson's novel *Meeting at a Far Meridian*, which was to be made in the USSR. (I had done some work on this project.) The Russians readily accepted my invitation to come to the Showcase, and seemed impressed by the quality of the acting, singing and dancing. But they were amazed, and indeed shocked, to learn that the students had to pay for their training. What an example of the evils of capitalism! I didn't tell them of the financial crisis at the school.

On the day of my move into my new home, I had another critical meeting with the Academy staff. Noel Behn had managed somehow to get together enough money for two of the five weeks' pay owing to us. There was no sign of a long-term solution, yet spirits remained admirably high. Sanford Meisner, much the highest paid member of staff, was urged by the Neighborhood Playhouse to return there; I was amazed that he didn't.

Meanwhile Sybil had found and settled into a spacious and attractive apartment. It was a great comfort to know that New York would be home for her and the children; I saw them frequently. But when *Cleopatra* opened she left town; she knew that the great Taylor–Burton scandal would be rife again. The film itself received mixed reviews, and Sybil called me from Chicago, where she seemed to be coping well with the situation. Later she went to California to visit her old friend Rachel Roberts. They needed to see each other to share their troubles. While she was away I was happy to keep an eye on the children, who had a good nurse, Liliana. One day, however, Sybil phoned me in distress about an article that had appeared in a London newspaper, the *News of the World*. She must have read it to me but I don't remember its contents. It had been written by Richard's younger brother Graham, and I was provoked into writing to him about it; I wondered if Richard would see my letter.

My new home was causing me trouble, financial, constructional and physical. A lot had to be done to it and I had some difficulty in finding a contractor who would guarantee me a Certificate of Occupancy. Christian worked tirelessly and I did my blundering best to help whenever I could, even spending nine hours one day stripping plaster from walls; that was certainly my lifetime record.

In late August Sybil and I saw Aaron Frosch in preparation for his forthcoming meeting with Richard to finalize the divorce settlement. On the same day I heard that Richard was going to play *Hamlet* on Broadway, and I foresaw trouble when I was told that Sir John Gielgud was to be the director; as I have already noted, their conceptions of the character were contradictory. Two weeks after our meeting with Aaron, Sybil had a this-is-the-end letter from Richard; there was no mention of me in it. I had long wondered how Ivor, Richard's brother, was adapting to the marital situation. I knew he couldn't approve of Richard's conduct and yet he couldn't leave him. Sybil heard that he had made his disapproval very clear.

During this period the Academy's financial problems grew steadily worse; ironically I knew that Richard would have been happy to help me, but I couldn't ask him. He was in Mexico, in Puerto Vallarta, working on the film *The Night of the Iguana*, and Elizabeth was with him. Aaron had gone there, and on 20 December he finalized the divorce of Richard and Sybil. My happiest memories of that Christmas are of being with the children, Grandpa trying to make up for the absence of Daddy. The one welcome Christmas surprise was that Richard sent a cable for me to Aaron's office. I was glad that he wanted to renew contact, but I wasn't sufficiently adjusted to the new situation even to acknowledge his message.

On the very last day of the year I did make one positive and important decision: I applied for American citizenship. After almost ten years in the USA, it was high time I ceased to be a Resident Alien.

CHAPTER Ten

The Academy came to an end as a commercial venture and became a non-profit-making enterprise – and my responsibility. I felt it was too good to be closed. A committee of determined ladies was formed to raise money to keep us going. The name was changed to the American Musical and Dramatic Academy (AMDA), and I became both President and Director. One of the first meetings of the Ladies' Committee took place in Sybil's apartment. The most difficult and reluctant decision I had to make was to tell Sanford Meisner that we could no longer afford him; he returned to the Neighborhood Playhouse. In order to demonstrate the new status of the Academy, its founder, Noel Behn, severed his official connection with AMDA, while I decided to do more teaching; in particular, I added a weekly lecture, given to the whole school, on dramatic literature. At one of my Rhetoric classes a student chose to read a short story which obviously ridiculed Richard. Could he have thought it would please me? I decided to ignore it and pass on to the next student. Later the offending student phoned me and offered a tearful apology.

In an effort to ensure AMDA's survival, a zealous member of the Ladies' Committee went behind my back to Aaron to ask him to get in touch with Richard and appeal to him for help. I was relieved to hear that Aaron had told the lady he couldn't pass on the message without my approval. Around this time I saw Richard on screen in the film *Becket*; his performance caused me to weep with pride. I just had to write to him about it, and I gave the letter to Aaron, who was flying to see Richard the following week. However, before he left I took it back. I was glad I had done so when I spent my usual Sunday afternoon with the children in the Park.

Richard was now in Toronto playing Hamlet at the O'Keefe Center in a production directed by Sir John Gielgud. This was a try-out engagement prior to Broadway. On Saturday 2 February I was having dinner with the Baruths when I received a phone call transferred from my house. To my great and somewhat unsettling surprise, because I had never met or spoken to her, it was Elizabeth Taylor. As I had anticipated, Richard was having trouble in *Hamlet*; he said I was the only one who could help him. Would I come up? Not for the first time in the two-year silence of separation, I was torn in my loyalties. Then Richard came on the line, and that soon settled it. I said I would come the following Saturday. When I later spoke to Sybil about it, she said, 'Of course you must go; he needs you.' I think that incident bears testimony to the fine qualities of both Elizabeth and Sybil.

Richard couldn't meet me at the airport because a matinée was in progress. I was taken to the theatre and to his dressing room. I both longed for and dreaded our meeting, but it turned out to be quite remarkable; we both behaved as though it had just been too long since we had seen each other: there was no embarrassment. When the matinée was over we went to the hotel suite. After a nervous delay, Elizabeth came out to meet me. Although it was a tentative meeting on both sides, it was a good one, and it was to lead to a warm and enduring friendship. I was to discover that her character, values, intelligence and talent matched her famous beauty.

That evening I saw *Hamlet*. In her original call Elizabeth had asked me to go to a performance with her, but subsequently, and I think rightly, it had been decided that I should go alone. Richard had been so nervous about my reaction that he had had difficulty in deciding where I should sit and had changed my ticket several times. The result was that when he wanted me – and he did – he didn't know where I was sitting. After the first act, the intermission dragged on and on, and people began to stamp their feet. Then into the auditorium came Hume Cronin, the actor playing Polonius. He was wearing a dressing gown and was looking for someone. I thought it might be me and I stood up. Hume beckoned me and I went to him. Richard was in such a state that he couldn't go on without a word from me, so I gave him one, and a very strong one. This was so unlike Richard that I have come to believe it couldn't have happened; I must have dreamed it.

The production was conceived as a rehearsal run-through; the only advantage I could see in this was that it saved the expense of period costumes. The Ghost was never seen; it was just a recorded voice, the inimitable one of Sir John Gielgud himself. As I expected, Richard's Hamlet lacked confidence because of the conflict between his conception of the part and Gielgud's.

Back in the hotel the three of us had a brief meeting and then Elizabeth retired so that Richard and I could talk about his performance, for that was the main purpose of my visit. As usual in such circumstances we talked for hours. I gave him detailed comments and suggestions, but my main purpose was to restore his confidence. I couldn't see another performance in Toronto because I had a very important appointment on the Monday. That Sunday I waited in my room for a call but it didn't come until 4 p.m. It seemed I had failed to reassure him, and he had not gone to bed until 7 a.m. I did my best to repair any damage I might unwittingly have caused, but I later realized that he had spent the time in absorbing my suggestions. It was a great relief to get a phone call from Hume Cronin after my return to New York. 'What did you do?' he asked. 'He gave a wonderful performance last night. We're all talking about it. It's put new life into the show.'

My very important appointment on Monday 2 March was the ceremony at which I was sworn in as a citizen of the USA. In order to gain American citizenship I had had to undergo an interview and examination. My examiner proved to be an amiable young man, probably new to the job. He had a surprisingly large file on me, and two things in it worried him. The first had to do with Richard. Some member of Congress had been so upset by the public liaison with Elizabeth that he wanted to bar them both from ever setting foot in the USA again. I said to the examiner that I didn't approve of it either, but what could I do? 'Would you visit the sins of the children on the father?' I asked, but my witticism was lost on him. The second difficulty was that I had been awarded an MBE (Mil) by King George VI. This implied loyalty to a foreign country, which I would have to disclaim. I told him I was reluctant to do so and would be grateful if he would get another opinion. He readily agreed and left the room. After a few minutes he returned smiling. I could keep my decoration because there was a precedent for it: General MacArthur had been a general in the Philippine army!

There were about two hundred of us being admitted to citizenship, and the judge who conducted the ceremony made it most memorable. His theme was that in becoming Americans we should bring with us the best of the cultures in which we had been reared. As he left the platform his last words were, 'May this day bring you rich blessings, and I don't mean material ones.'

In the evening there was a delightful party to honour the new American citizen. It was held in the apartment of my Academy secretary, which had been appropriately decorated by Christian. As we entered we were greeted by a large placard proclaiming *PHILIP BURTON for PRESIDENT*, but that, fortunately, would require a fundamental change in the Constitution. Christian had also set the rules for the evening: everyone was invited to bring a gift costing not more than a dollar – this was to prevent embarrassment for those with little money – and a poem written by themselves. With my encouragement, my secretary later became a professional actress, and now she is well known to television viewers; her name is Katherine Helmond. Her husband, David Christian, was also encouraged by me – but to do the opposite, to abandon his proposed acting career for one in art, in which he is very talented. A photograph of a bust he made of me is reproduced on the dust jacket of my book *The Sole Voice*.

Again I had to share the parlous financial condition of AMDA with the staff, and again they were inspiringly supportive. I alternated between regret at having undertaken the battle to save the school, and excitement at the challenge, although Sanford Meisner was less optimistic and kept urging me to close AMDA.

Of course I had given Sybil an account of my visit to Toronto; she fully appreciated my ambivalent position. Then we heard that on 15 March Richard and Elizabeth had got married in Montreal. Again Sybil's reaction was admirable; it was the end of the chapter. But she decided to leave town in early April because of the imminent arrival of *Hamlet*. I should miss her and the children very much.

On 3 April Richard called me from Boston; he wanted me to go there to see the play again. I went the next day by train, and again arrived while he was at a matinée, but this time I was taken to his hotel and had a meeting with the new Mrs Burton before Richard came back from the theatre. That evening's performance, the last before Broadway, was a joyous relief; the whole production was much improved and Richard was electrifying. There was no need for a late note-giving session; instead the three of us had dinner together. I wanted Richard to help raise money for AMDA and asked if he would give a poetry recital for the benefit of the school. He readily agreed; then, to my great surprise, he added, 'Why don't you ask Elizabeth too?' The idea had never occurred to me but, when I asked her, she said she would, on condition I coached her! I was astonished. She had never performed on a public stage; what courage it would take to do so, especially before the audience we could expect! But what an attraction for an AMDA benefit!

The next day the three of us caught the one o'clock train, with the help of innumerable police. In New York we were met by squads of yet more police, who escorted us to the Regency Hotel. Later I saw a rough cut of a television interview Richard had given about *Hamlet*, in which he made some very flattering references to me. The first night of *Hamlet* lived up to my high hopes for it, and was followed by a very happy party in the

Rainbow Room. Then came the notices. As I confidently expected, they were excellent for Richard, but there were one or two quibbles about the production.

There was great excitement both in the Academy and among the Ladies' Committee at the promised joint appearance of Richard and Elizabeth for the benefit of AMDA, but I couldn't begin to deal with that yet, since I was abnormally busy. I was still teaching at the school and some days I lectured for as much as six hours. Moreover, I now became involved in a commercial television project, a very interesting one, although I doubted from the beginning that it could be a popular success. It was to be a weekly series of hour-long shows, and the title finally chosen for it was *The Human Stage*. Each week the subject would be a well-known play. I was to choose, direct and introduce the show, and following my introduction a significant scene from the play would be shown. This would in turn be followed by a discussion arising from the subject of the play. I would lead the discussion at which some invited expert would be present to take part with the cast. The show would end with another scene from the play, again introduced by me. The first play I chose was Ibsen's *Ghosts*, in which Mildred Dunnock was to play Mrs Alving and Christian was to play Oswald. The second subject was to be Strindberg's *The Father* and the third *Frankenstein*, for which I found Edward Carmel, who suffered from gigantism, to play the Monster. He had spent most of his life on display in side shows at circuses and fairs, and was so enormous that the rings on his fingers were sold as bracelets. He seemed to me a tragic figure; for instance, taxi drivers were so scared by his appearance that they would rarely stop for him, and yet he had difficulty in walking any distance. To my relief and surprise I found him to be intelligent and sensitive. He was perfect casting for the Monster, who in the original story by Mary Shelley enlists our sympathy; but could I get him to act? I had evening sessions with him at my house, and Christian came to help by playing the other parts. One evening we were rehearsing a scene in which the Monster throttles a victim who is kneeling in front of him. I was standing close to Ed and speaking to him; he towered above me and I'm not short. I had foolishly assumed that he knew the trick of stage strangulation, in which all the pressure is put on the back of the neck. I was pleased by the energy he was exerting until a loud gurgle drew my attention to Christian, who was really being strangled. The nervous and physical strain on Ed Carmel during the rehearsals and filming was tremendous, but he did well, and later spoke in the televised discussion of the social isolation to which his physical difference condemned him.

On a Saturday in mid-April Richard and Elizabeth paid their first visit to my house. With them were Cis and Elfed, who were over on holiday. I'm sure that Cis had had little difficulty in adjusting to the change in Richard's married life; all that mattered to her was his happiness, and if Elizabeth was necessary to that, so be it. She undoubtedly frowned on divorce as such, but for her Richard was a law unto himself. On that morning he was not well, and he had two performances ahead of him. He was unable to take part in the house tour or to eat the lunch I had prepared. But in spite of this, the visit was a very happy one.

On the following Monday I had two preparatory meetings, both of which resulted in my sharing a stage with Richard. The first had to do with Dylan Thomas. The sculptor David Slivka had taken a death mask of Dylan and from it had made an excellent bronze head, of which I think there were four copies. 'Artists of America', but chiefly Paul Jenkins, had bought one to be presented to the National Museum of Wales. I was asked to arrange and preside at a ceremony at the Poetry Center, when the bust would be presented to Richard, who would represent the Museum. Dylan himself had been well known for his appearances on the stage on which the ceremony would take place. The sculptor allowed me to buy one of the bronzes, which I gave as a wedding present to Richard and Elizabeth.

I was unusually nervous at the actual ceremony at the Poetry Center, probably because I was tired from overwork. Present onstage with Richard and me were David Slivka, Nancy Wickwire, who had taken part with Dylan Thomas in the original reading of *Under Milk Wood* on that stage, John Malcolm

Brinnin, who had been responsible for first bringing Dylan to the USA, and, of course, the bronze head itself. In the front row of the audience, very appropriately, was Alec Guinness, who was at that time playing Dylan on Broadway in a play about the poet. I think Dylan would have been gratified by the evening.

The other important preparatory meeting that Monday was an elaborate press conference at the Regency Hotel to announce formally the forthcoming poetry recital. Elizabeth had agreed to take part in the conference, so we had a full house. She told me she was very nervous but you wouldn't have thought so; she acquitted herself superbly. I started to work with her in the evenings when Richard was at the theatre. The first problem was her total reliance on a microphone, since film actors have no audience to command by their presence. Now she had to learn to project, even though there would be a microphone, and to speak consciously to a large audience sitting in front of her. I sat as far away as I could when she read; again I was reminded of my mountain exercises with Richard. I think she knew she would surprise me when I asked her if there was any particular poem she would like to read, because she replied rather defiantly, 'Yes. "The Leaden Echo and the Golden Echo".' I had once described this poem by Gerard Manley Hopkins as the single most difficult poem in the English language to speak, because it depends so much on the sounds of the words and the rhythm of the lines. It was for this very reason that I had worked on it with Richard twenty years before. I didn't know that he had frequently used it as one of his private show-off pieces. I was reluctant to agree to Elizabeth's doing it, but gradually she proved to me that she could, and in the performance she brought it off triumphantly. When Richard spoke the lines

> How to keep ...
> Back beauty, keep it, beauty, beauty, beauty, ... from vanishing away?

it was a philosophical question, but with Elizabeth it became a deeply personal one. I had arranged for them to do a few things together, but he didn't hear her solo items until the actual evening, and in an aside after one of her readings he brought the house down by saying, 'I didn't think she would be as good as this.' One of the items he enjoyed sharing was the 23rd Psalm. After I had introduced it, they recited in turn each verse, she in English and he in his beloved Welsh.

The recital was a sensational success. The theatre world and the film world were there in force, astonished by Elizabeth's performance. They had expected her to be a limp second in support of Richard, but she stole the show. No one was more surprised and delighted than Richard. Elizabeth had never faced a theatre audience before – and what an audience! – and she had total command of it. A memorable comment on the evening came from Beatrice Lillie; it was reported to me by Emlyn Williams. When the show had been going for half an hour she said to her companion, 'If she doesn't get worse soon, they'll be leaving.' After all expenses had been paid the Academy benefited by $25,000.

Working together enabled Elizabeth and me to get to know and appreciate each other. Then I also met her family, her parents when they stopped off in New York on their way to Europe, and her children when they came to stay with her. I took the two boys, Michael and Christopher Wilding, to a matinée of *Hamlet*. The play prevented Richard from accompanying Elizabeth to a special showing in the Philharmonic Hall of the film *The Night of the Iguana*. I went with her and Montgomery Clift. While Richard had been working on the film in Puerto Vallarta, he and Elizabeth had bought a house there. As we watched the film, Elizabeth kept whispering to me about the place, pointing out what was off-screen in relation to what we could see. She and Monty Clift were obviously very close friends. I enjoyed being with them, and two weeks afterwards we met again, this time for dinner at Monty's house. In my diary I commented: 'He's a strange man but I warm to him.' Two years later Monty died; it was a sad loss for Elizabeth.

I also accompanied Elizabeth and her two sons to Philadelphia to see Sammy Davis in *Golden Boy*. (At Sammy's request I had gone down previously to see the show and had given him extensive notes on it; he was so impressed by them that, to my intense embarrassment, he had insisted on my repeating them to the director and the producer.) We went to Philadelphia by car but returned by train because Elizabeth enjoys train travel so much; the car came back empty of passengers. I learned something on that trip, although Richard had already warned me about it; Elizabeth is never on time. We were half an hour late in getting to the theatre; they had held the curtain for twenty minutes. Subsequently, if we had an appointment I would tell her it was half an hour earlier than it was.

On 6 August Richard's Hamlet broke the Broadway record, and to mark the occasion it was filmed; two days later it closed. To celebrate the record-breaking performance there was a large party at Voisin's, but Richard, Elizabeth and I shared a cosy table. I went to see *Hamlet* on the following two nights as well: on the Friday chiefly to hear Hume Cronin's speech about breaking the record, and on the Saturday because it was almost certainly the last time I would see Richard as Hamlet; he was fittingly on the top of his form. Of course there was another big late-night party; I didn't get to bed until 4.30 a.m., which in recent years has become the time I get up. The following Tuesday the family left town for California.

The very next day I got a warm message from Sybil by way of a mutual friend; I hadn't heard from her since our last meeting. She followed the message with a letter. On 29 September she and the girls returned to the New York apartment; it was good to have them back. The following day I resumed the happy expeditions with the children to the Park; Kate was now seven and Jessica two months short of five. Soon afterwards I was surprised by a phone call from California. It was Elizabeth's mother, who had been instructed by her daughter to tell me that she, Richard, Michael and Christopher were on their way back to New York. That night I met them, but the reunion was not as happy as I had hoped for; Richard was rather high and Elizabeth tearfully guilty about Sybil and the girls.

The next day Sybil readily agreed that Richard should see

Kate and Jessica, but she herself wouldn't be present. I was there to welcome him. Kate was overjoyed to see him, but was later saddened that her mother hadn't been there too. Jessica seemed not to know her father and clung to me; she had long had a strong attachment to me. Richard and I took the girls to F.O. Schwartz's, a children's paradise. Richard's stay in New York was brief; they were soon on their way home to Europe. Elizabeth called me from Paris to urge me to spend Christmas with them in Switzerland. I couldn't commit myself because I had so many obligations ahead, and it turned out that I couldn't go.

Almost immediately after that call came one from Sybil; she was worried on account of little Jessica and wanted my help. Of course I went over immediately, and was able to calm Jessica. She was beautiful and physically very active, but she couldn't speak. I used to try to comfort Sybil by telling her that Einstein couldn't speak until he was seven. Sometimes Jessica would express her frustration by destructive tantrums and, tragically, it turned out that the little girl was autistic and would always need special care. What an added burden for Sybil! Richard saw to it that Jessica was well provided for, and would have that care for the rest of her life.

CHAPTER
Eleven

In January of 1965 Ivor and Gwen came to stay with Sybil for a month. Ivor had adjusted to the new situation as I had; if Richard needed Elizabeth as his wife, that didn't affect our loyalty to Sybil and the children. I was personally very glad that Ivor and Gwen were in New York because I was absurdly busy, often working at the Academy for twelve hours a day. I was so busy that the visitors never saw my house. I was rehearsing three shows at the same time, in addition to teaching and lecturing.

I had become so tired of the school that I needed a change, and agreed to run a summer theatre in Clinton, New Jersey. It would help AMDA in that I would not take my salary during the summer, but would go back to visit the school one day every week. When things eased enough, I was happy to fulfil a request of Richard's. He wanted me to buy a library of books for him, to be sent to the house in Puerto Vallarta. The choice was to be mine because I knew what books he would want. What a delightful assignment for a bibliophile like me! Perhaps 'bibliomaniac' would be nearer the mark. I continued to go to the Park with the children, although sometimes I would take only Jessica. As soon as she saw me she would run to me and make it quite clear that we should go for a walk. As for Kate, she was beginning to need my help with her school work, especially arithmetic.

In an attempt to get more free time, I told the SSDC Committee that I would not run for a third two-year term in office.

Important and necessary as the work was, it had taken up a great deal of my time, and some of it had been exhausting.

AMDA was in one financial crisis after another; I could never relax about it. Now it was Dina Merrill, a good friend of mine, who gave us a temporary respite by becoming guarantor for a bank loan of $15,000. And hanging over my head was the threat that I would be personally responsible for the unpaid taxes that the school had incurred in the days when it was a commercial enterprise. This was the result of a document that Noel Behn had got me to sign; I had understood it to be a mere formality, the more fool I. Every time I heard of the claim, interest had made it grow alarmingly. I had to live with this threat for ten years. Aaron frequently tried to get my alleged responsibility cancelled, and he finally succeeded in 1975.

I was also having difficulty in paying my personal income tax because some money I had counted on had not materialized; nor was the duplex apartment in the house rented. Many people had seen it and all had seemed to like it, but it didn't fit their needs or they didn't like the district. It was almost two and a half years after I first bought the house that I found perfect tenants: Charles Mee and his wife and daughter.

After a largely successful summer season in Clinton, I came back for the new term at the Academy. Soon I was as busy as ever, but I still found time to add a new activity: the lecture circuit under the management of Colston-Leigh. This was to grow into a major source of income in preparation for my retirement years. My first engagement was in Springfield, Massachusetts, and it was a joint appearance with Christian. I called it *A Pageant of Kings*, since it dealt with Shakespeare's kings of England, about whom he wrote ten plays. My lecture was illustrated by enacted scenes in which Christian played the younger parts. The response from our audiences could hardly have been better.

My second lecture was in the evening at the easily accessible Monmouth College, and it too became a popular one. I gave it the title *The Miracle That Was Shakespeare*. Giving a public lecture for the first time is a great strain on the nerves, and I had to follow it the next day with six hours of teaching. I was so exhausted by the end of that day that I didn't want even to eat, which in me is a serious warning sign.

At the annual meeting of the SSDC on 1 November I was relieved to give up office, but I had been persuaded to give a talk entitled *Shakespeare and the Director*. The meeting went on so long that I hoped I could beg off, but they insisted on hearing me. I remained in close touch with the Society as a member of the Board, without executive responsibility. Even so, I found my duties as a Board member too demanding, and after another three years I declined to run for re-election. I remain on the stationery in the list of Honorary Advisors, and still take a lively interest in the work of the Society.

I had arranged to make a brief lecture tour with Christian, but before I left I found time to say goodbye to Kate, who was back in town with her mother. To my delight, Sybil had that June become Mrs Jordan Christopher, though her marriage was to rob me of her valued presence in New York. One Saturday morning Kate came to the Academy with me and thoroughly enjoyed watching a dancing class as she sat on my lap. It was now quite safe to leave the school in the hands of Joyce Worsley, the very capable Registrar, as I had in the summer. After appearing with Christian in three states, I made some solo appearances in *The Miracle That Was Shakespeare* and *The Magic of Poetry*, before joining up again with Christian in New Orleans and Miami. We stayed with friends in Florida, and on Thanksgiving Day they drove us down to see Key West. I found it to be an enchanting place and was determined to return. Ultimately and happily it became my last home town.

In the following year, lecture tours became an increasing part of my life. The activity was pleasurable, stimulating and profitable. Christian shared some engagements with me in that first season, but thereafter I was alone. Fortunately I was often invited back and so my list of lectures grew. In addition to those already mentioned I offered *Comedy through the Ages*, *A Gallery of Eccentrics*, *A Portrait of Hamlet*, *The Theatre of the Absurd*, and lectures on *Macbeth* and *King Lear*. I must have lectured in almost all the forty-eight contiguous states, as well as Canada and Mexico. In addition to touring myself, I formed two companies of former students, called the Philip Burton Players. The first presented *The Battle of the Sexes*, a series of scenes from famous plays, together with *Art Thou Not Romeo?*, which consisted of skits I had devised showing how the Balcony scene from *Romeo and Juliet* might have been written by Noël Coward, Bernard Shaw, Eugene O'Neill and Edward Albee. The second company played *Set to Music*, which was a series of numbers from musicals; on the stage with them there had to be a grand piano – and a grand pianist.

After the first brief lecture tour I resumed my full schedule at the Academy. Some of the staff and the Ladies' Committee had been busy with preparations for what became the annual bazaar. I always felt guilty that I didn't do more to help, but Joyce did more than enough to make up for me, and I was kept busy for eleven hours on the day of the bazaar itself. Some graduates and senior students put on an entertainment which made me proud of AMDA.

One professional activity of mine that fall came as a total surprise to me. Franco Zeffirelli, with whom I had become friends, was directing the world premiere at the new Lincoln Center Opera House of Samuel Barber's *Antony and Cleopatra*. The company was having difficulty with some of the text, and Franco asked me to come in and help. He himself was not only directing but had also designed the elaborate production, and much of his time was taken in dealing with the technical problems of the staging. I was given a contract and enjoyed working with the cast, particularly Leontyne Price.

In December of that year I saw Richard in a preview of *The Spy Who Came in from the Cold*; it was a happy occasion after the embarrassment of *The Sandpiper*, a depressingly bad film which he had recently made with Elizabeth.

In the new year Richard and Elizabeth were again involved in the financial troubles of AMDA. I was reluctant to approach them a second time but was persuaded to do so, the object being to get a benefit preview of their latest film *Who's Afraid of*

Virginia Woolf? They agreed and got in touch with Jack Warner in Hollywood. The preview was arranged for Thursday 23 January, Jack Warner himself promising to be present. It was known from the beginning that Richard and Elizabeth could not be there, so to glamorize the evening we decided to end it with a supper ball. There was one unexpected complication. Richard had recently been diagnosed as having a tendency towards haemophilia; it was not serious and never became so, but the report had received some publicity. Quite rightly, the Hemophilia Foundation had appealed to Richard for help, with the result that the proceeds of the benefit were to be shared between AMDA and the Foundation. While AMDA was waiting for its share of the proceeds, two members of the Board of Directors came forward with $5,000 each to keep the school open.

The *Virginia Woolf* benefit was a great success, and I was relieved that I could be genuinely enthusiastic about Richard's performance. When the material was good and challenging, he and Elizabeth made a superb team. He once told me, 'You taught me all I know about theatre, but Elizabeth taught me film acting.'

The supper ball after the film turned into a near-disaster when the air conditioning broke down, together with the microphones and some of the lights; people left in droves. Nonetheless, Jack Warner kept his promise to be present, for which I was grateful. Our initial contact over the phone had been promising, and a mutual appreciation was confirmed by our face-to-face meeting.

I sent a cable to Richard and Elizabeth about the film, and they were so moved by it that they called me up from Rome. Then Elizabeth completed the benefit by establishing an AMDA scholarship in her name.

In early January 1967 Aaron went to Rome to see Richard and Elizabeth, and came back with a pressing invitation from them for me to go to London for the royal premiere of their film of *The Taming of the Shrew*. I just couldn't take the time off, although Aaron and his wife went. About a week later I saw a preview of the film in New York, but in this case I was unexpectedly disappointed by Richard's performance.

In March I was invited to go to Washington, DC to promote a new and exciting project: Shakespeare in the Park, the park being the one containing the Washington Monument, a wonderful site for a large open-air theatre. I had a delightful meeting with the Secretary of the Interior, Stewart Udall, and then a three-hour luncheon meeting with three Washington theatre critics. I wasn't very surprised when later in the month I was asked to direct the play that would initiate the project. It was to open in early July and run for six weeks. The theatre would have an audience capacity of 5,000 and all performances were to be free but, to help meet expenses, there would be a small charge of one and two dollars for the front seats. Because of the potential for vast audiences, the organizers wanted a comedy, but if they wanted me it had to be *Hamlet*. Somewhat reluctantly they agreed. Among the established professional actors who had worked with me I had sensed a Hamlet in Robert Drivas, and he proved me right. Christian was bitterly disappointed that I didn't choose him, but he didn't have the credits to satisfy our backers; besides, I felt he had had too little stage experience as an actor to take on the challenge and the burden of the part, especially in such difficult physical conditions. I have since thought I may have been wrong to deny him the supreme opportunity, but he had to be satisfied with Laertes. I longed to see his Hamlet some day, but that longing was never to be satisfied.

I have described in my book *Early Doors* how in spite of rain, aeroplanes overhead from the National Airport, the 72-foot-wide stage, etc., etc., the play was a big success. So impressed were the organizers that they wanted me back the following year to direct and play the title role in *King Lear*. I was tempted but declined; I had discussed it with Richard and he was strongly against my playing the part under such conditions. Instead, I did a production of *Romeo and Juliet* in which the Montagues were all white and the Capulets were all black, thus making Tybalt a black activist. It turned out, not by design, that the cast of forty-two were exactly divided into white and black. There were many more Blacks in the audiences than were expected; it was the summer of Resurrection City, a large camp of protesting Blacks, brought together in Washington, DC in reaction to the assassination of Martin Luther King three months before.

To return to the *Hamlet* year, 1967. I decided to close the Academy for the summer because the registration for the summer school was too small. As always, we were in serious financial trouble. The benefit that year, *An Evening with the Stars*, was an outstanding artistic success but disappointing financially. After a discussion with Aaron, we decided I should ask Richard for $15,000 of which $10,000 was to be a loan. The help was immediately forthcoming. Many impractical fund-raising suggestions came from well-wishers, for example a North African tour of *Oklahoma* played by AMDA graduates, and a Philip Burton school in Hollywood.

Two important changes in my life took place in September 1967. I sold my house and moved into a very pleasant apartment on Riverside Drive. I made no money from the sale of the house – had I held on to it for a few years I should have made a lot – but it was proving to be too big for me; some of the rooms were never used. I had lived there for four years and four months. The second change was more significant. William Decker, a senior editor at Dial Press, persuaded me to write an autobiographical book, but I restricted it, in the words of the subtitle, to 'My Life and the Theatre'. All my previous writing had been for broadcasting or for the theatre, but Bill Decker launched me into a new activity, one that still absorbs me twenty-five years later. My original title for my first book was *The Reluctant Teacher*, because, without meaning to, I always ended up teaching, but Bill preferred one he had found in the text of the book, *Early Doors*. It was a phrase taken from my early theatre-going, when the doors to the pit and gallery were opened an hour before the performance, and you paid a little extra for having the first choice of seats; if the show was popular, there would be no seats left when 'ordinary doors' were opened at the half-hour at standard prices. It was two years before *Early Doors* was published because my heavy obligations left me little time for writing. It was dedicated 'To R. and E. with love'.

In October Richard paid back the cultural debt he owed to Neville Coghill and Oxford University by appearing there in a benefit production of Marlowe's *Doctor Faustus* for the Oxford University Dramatic Society (OUDS). To enhance its already assured success he persuaded Elizabeth to play the non-speaking part of Helen of Troy. I'm sure Richard remembered the time, more than twenty years before, when we worked on the role of Faustus in that garden in Stratford-upon-Avon. He and Elizabeth wanted me to go to the opening, but my engagements prevented it; however, I joined them in Rome for a week at the end of the month. The production of *Doctor Faustus* had been filmed, and Richard arranged to have the film flown over from London so that I could see it. The supporting cast were all members of OUDS, amateurs, so I hadn't expected too much from the production as a whole, judged by professional standards. In fact I was very pleasantly surprised, so much so that I asked if I could have the film for a benefit showing for AMDA. Elizabeth's impact on the film in her brief and silent appearance was such that Helen of Troy would have been jealous of her. Richard and Elizabeth not only agreed to my having the film but said they would be present at the benefit if it could be arranged in early February, when they would be in New York on their way back from Hollywood. They were going there to make the film *Boom*, an adaptation of the play by Tennessee Williams, *The Milk Train Doesn't Stop Here Any More*.

I was very reluctant to leave Rome, but manifold duties called. As soon as I got back I told Liska March, my very efficient liaison with the Ladies' Committee, about the *Doctor Faustus* film and Richard and Elizabeth's promise to be present at the benefit, which would be the only occasion on which the film could be seen publicly; after all, it was only a film of a staged play. In no time at all we had booked the Philharmonic Hall for 6 February.

Richard arrived in New York with Elizabeth and for the first time in many years I had dinner with him on his birthday, his forty-second. AMDA was having another financial crisis, and again the Board considered closing the school before deciding to try to keep it going. After all, *Doctor Faustus* lay ahead. The annual bazaar made less than usual but Aaron Frosch himself came to the immediate rescue with an outright donation of $10,000 and the promise of another $10,000 the following year.

The benefit on 6 February was a great success. The high spot was the entrance of Richard and Elizabeth, which caused a near-riot, if that word can be used for the conduct of such a distinguished audience. But my personal high spot was a meeting with Bobby Kennedy. Richard had spoken to him about me and he had said he wanted to meet me. We got on so well together that he asked me to visit him and his family in Washington; he particularly wanted me to meet a son about whom he needed some advice. We met again in New York but not at his home in Washington; an assassin prevented that.

In August Richard and Elizabeth were again in New York for a few days, but Elizabeth was far from well – she had had a hysterectomy which proved to be more complicated than expected – and Richard was in a bad mood for much of the time. He had read a draft copy of *Early Doors* and while he approved of some of it, particularly a chapter on Shakespeare, he disapproved of much more; for example, what had happened to my sense of humour? He said he had made ten pages of notes but had forgotten to bring them with him. I never saw them. Naturally I was disappointed by his reaction, but my editor, Bill Decker, persuaded me to ignore it, which wasn't easy.

Meanwhile AMDA was having a new kind of crisis. We had to move out of the perfect building on 23rd Street because it was being demolished. Months and months were spent in looking for a new home and several times we thought we had found one, only to be robbed of it during the negotiations: the originally quoted rent would rise out of reach; the Building Code would not allow the use of the place as a school; for some unstated reason the landlord would change his mind about letting us have it. After an exhausting search and many disappointments we decided to rent the seventeenth floor of the Hotel Martinique. We moved in over a weekend and classes started on Tuesday 1 October. But our new home lasted for only nine months; fire regulations forced us to move. Next we found a place on Bleecker Street, but the move there was delayed for another nine months by the landlord's difficulties in getting a Certificate of Occupancy. Slowly, however, we got a good deal of work done in adapting the premises to our requirements.

One bright spot at that difficult time was the discovery that Agnes de Mille had agreed to write a foreword to my book. We had first met nine years before in the early days of the Society of Stage Directors and Choreographers, and no one did more to establish the rights of choreographers than she. I had found her to be not only brilliant and innovative at her profession but a stimulating and enchanting companion; her artistic eye was matched with an acute intelligence and a lively wit. When I lived in New York I enjoyed many a dinner at Agnes's home with her and her husband, Walter Prude, and summer weekends at Merriewold, their country retreat. In 1975, as she was about to make a public appearance with her dance troupe, she suffered a very severe stroke. For most people this would have been the end of their career, but for Agnes it was a new challenge. Since that time she has suffered additional cardiac and neurological attacks, but her indomitable spirit has triumphed so that she has not only added to her impressive list of books, but has made public appearances, particularly on television, her first-class mind unimpaired. She is a truly remarkable human being, and I feel privileged to be one of her friends.

In January 1969 I officially resigned as Director of AMDA. Joyce Worsley took my place, but I continued to teach and give lectures at the school, and to take my share in dealing with its problems, such as getting the City's permission for the move to Bleecker Street. Nonetheless, it was a joy to feel free to dawdle on my next lecture tour, which took me all over the country, as well as to Mexico City. (I had considerable difficulty in getting a Mexican visa because I was going to earn money there.) On my return from Mexico I spent two weeks with friends in Florida and made a second visit to Key West, the 'Island Paradise', which only enhanced the impression made on me by the first.

Another sign of my new freedom was that I began work on

another book, one that I knew Richard would heartily approve of. It was to be my view of twenty-one of Shakespeare's characters, seven each from the Histories, the Comedies and the Tragedies. The title I hit on was *The Sole Voice*, from Matthew Arnold's sonnet about Shakespeare, the last three lines of which are:

> All pains the immortal spirit must endure,
> All weakness that impairs, all griefs that bow,
> Find their sole voice in that victorious brow.

Yet a third advantage of my new comparative freedom was that I was able to spend time with my niece Megan and her husband Fred when they came from Wales for a two-week visit. They knew Richard very well from the years when he first became a Burton, for we had spent several weekends and holidays with the family in Mountain Ash. Richard had a particular rapport with my half-brother, Will Wilson, Megan's father. Will was the kind of colourful Welsh coal-mining character that Richard enjoyed, and he was also a very genuine theatre enthusiast; I had profited from that too. When he was a young man, Will would work a day shift underground, then stay down the mine for the following night shift. This would enable him to go to Cardiff by train to see a matinée featuring the great stars of those days such as Sir Johnston Forbes-Robertson or Sir John Martin-Harvey. He would go in by 'early doors' and fall asleep in his seat after asking the person sitting next to him to wake him when the show began.

My book *Early Doors* was on sale long before its official publication date, 5 May. To my surprise, its publication and reception did not give me as much satisfaction as the actual writing had done. I found this to be true for my other books, too. I wonder if other authors feel the same way. Of course I was interested in the press reviews, but not as much as the publishers were; I didn't feel my life depended on them as so many theatre and film people do – a performance is fleeting, a book persists. But I was deeply disappointed when some manuscripts of mine failed to achieve publication, because that is the completion of the process. After *Early Doors* appeared I also made several publicity tours, which I didn't enjoy at all, in sharp contrast to my lecture tours.

None of this prepared me for the crisis in my life that began on 2 September of that year. I was exhausted after climbing the stairs to the AMDA office, and my appearance must have worried Joyce Worsley because she told me to call my doctor at once. I reluctantly did so, only to discover he was on vacation; his answering service referred me to a doctor on Central Park South. At Joyce's insistence I rang this number and was given an immediate appointment. When the doctor had examined me he said that I was suffering from angina pectoris. I knew someone who had that and it didn't seem to trouble her unduly, so, since I was feeling no pain, I dismissed it. That evening I had a prearranged dinner with Christian at a restaurant on 72nd Street, only five blocks from where I lived. After the meal I had severe pains in the chest but very foolishly insisted on walking home. That wasn't the end of my folly. I refused to let Christian stay the night with me, and it became a night of agony. I assumed I was having gall-bladder trouble; only recently I had learned that I had large gallstones. By the morning my right arm was somewhat paralysed. I called the doctor and again he agreed to see me at once, but to make matters worse I walked part of the way to his office. After a brief examination he left the room and soon returned to tell me that he had arranged for me to be admitted to Mount Sinai Hospital; I wasn't even to go home to get anything. He didn't call an ambulance, probably to avoid scaring me unduly, but when I got outside it was raining and I couldn't find a taxi. I started to walk to the hospital but this became so painful that I was unable to continue. When I finally arrived at Mount Sinai I mumbled something, but all the receptionist caught was 'Burton'. She said, 'Yes, where is he? We've got the police out looking for him.' Only then did I realize that I must be in a critical condition. I was. When I recovered I was told that my survival had been a miracle.

CHAPTER
Twelve

After only six days in the intensive-care unit I was moved to a private room because somebody's life depended upon his getting my IC bed. The move set me back a little but soon I was well on the road to recovery. As I expected, I had far too many visitors, although it was always good to see them, and their concern for me was endearing. Unfortunately Richard and Elizabeth were only represented by beautiful flowers. I couldn't even speak to them; I wasn't allowed a phone.

Apparently my recovery was faster than originally expected; I was in hospital for a total of only four weeks. But then what? Since I lived alone, the doctors assumed I would go to a convalescent home, and preliminary arrangements had been made for me to do so, but I stubbornly insisted on staying in my apartment. Who was to look after me? Christian wasn't available. Finally it was decided that two former students of mine would share the care of me. To welcome me home were more flowers from Richard and Elizabeth.

I wasn't as well as I thought I was, and I started work at my desk far too soon. This with too many, but most welcome, visitors did me no good, and my doctor insisted on a strict regimen. The most distressing loss was that I had to cancel my lecture tours for November and December. A further unexpected impediment to my recovery was the noise of quarrelling in the apartment above mine; sometimes it kept me awake until 4 a.m. A complaint to the manager did little good; he merely apologized for the tenant's noisy new mistress. I suppose I should have taken the advice of the doctors and gone to a convalescent home.

Christmas was approaching and I had a great desire to spend it in Wales. My doctor agreed, provided I cancelled a planned lecture tour in January. Richard and Elizabeth gave me a first-class return flight for the trip. They came to New York on 17 December and I left on the 19th. It was a mercy that I was sufficiently recovered to enjoy thoroughly my two days with them. Particularly memorable was a private showing of the film *Anne of a Thousand Days*, concerning the rise and fall of Anne Boleyn. I was so thrilled by Richard's performance that I felt sure he would get an Oscar for it. It seems incredible that, in spite of several nominations through the years, he never got one. Apart from Richard's Henry VIII there was a special joy for me in the film: eleven-year-old Kate appeared with other children in a scene where they watched the King passing by.

Richard came to the AMDA Christmas party and, instead of my reading as usual Dylan Thomas's *A Child's Christmas in Wales*, he read his own *A Christmas Story*, an endearing evocation of his boyhood in Taibach with a moving tribute to his sister-mother, Cecilia, from which I quoted earlier. As a Christmas gift to AMDA students, he arranged for thirty of them to go to another private showing of *Anne of a Thousand Days*.

It seemed strange that it was I who left Richard and Elizabeth in New York, and not they me. Fred met me at London Airport and we drove down to Wales. They were now living outside Cardiff, in Llandaff. Fred was the headmaster of a high school in Newport, and Megan was a lecturer in a college. We had a perfect family Christmas Day, including going to the beautiful Llandaff Cathedral. During my stay I had yet another happy reunion with my old BBC friends, and Fred took me to Port Talbot.

While I was in Wales I did a good deal of work on what I thought was an amusing novel; certainly the writing of it amused me. I called it *The Layman*. It may seem strange that I should work when I needed to rest, but what I really needed was a complete change and a return to my roots. When I came back I intended to resume my old routine but I soon made two discoveries. The first was that directing a show took more out of me than lecturing. I was rehearsing, with the great assistance of Christian, the Philip Burton Players in *Set to Music*. It was deeply gratifying to learn that in their first engagement – it was in Toms River, New Jersey – they had received a five-minute standing ovation, but that didn't shake my resolution never to direct again. My second discovery was that I suffered badly in cold weather, and so my second resolution was never to spend another winter in New York; I would find a place in Florida, probably in Key West. In furtherance of that decision I spent the whole of February in Florida, staying very happily with friends in Tequesta, Coconut Grove and Key West, but without finding a home for the following winter.

To my surprise, Dial Press asked me if I would write a children's book; the idea would never have occurred to me. Then I remembered a wonderful old Welsh legend that I had heard when I was a teenager from that great New Testament scholar of Cambridge University, as great in person as he was in learning, C.H. Dodd. I set it on the west coast of Wales in Norman times, using the basic idea but adding a love story. My title for it was *The Green Isle*, and it was dedicated to Kate, as is this book. But the publishers aimed it at much too young an age group, thus missing the mark and the market. The beautiful illustrations by Robert Andrew Parker won a national award.

In March I tired myself out on a brief lecture tour in the Mid-West, although I suffered no lasting ill effects. But very soon something happened that did upset me, and Richard was the cause of it. It had been expected that he and Elizabeth (they were then in Hollywood) would come to the AMDA benefit on 26 April, but almost at the last moment they said they couldn't come, nor should their names be used. I suppose they felt that now that I was no longer the President and Director of the Academy they had no further obligation to it. What they hadn't realized was that the benefit was a testimonial to me on my retirement from the Academy. I was deeply hurt. I did not write or speak to them about it, but someone must have told them my reaction and the personal implications of the evening for me, because they said that, if it were postponed to 14 May, they would come. This offer came too late, but I was against accepting it anyhow. As I reflect on it now, I realize that my reactions and behaviour were very petty. On the night of the testimonial benefit in the Park Hotel, Richard's place on my right at the dinner table was taken by Sir Noël Coward. A special chorus had been composed for the occasion and it was sung with moving fervour by a group of students. The words were written by John Jury, who had helped take care of me when I came home from hospital, and the music was by Sam Pottle. The title was 'One Man'. Here are some of the lyrics. I quote them not in praise of myself, but to show both the challenge and the reward of teaching. It was sad that my most famous student was absent.

> One man whose star has touched so many,
> Made them glow, helped them to be bright,
> He'll never know how much, how many,
> Have grown and prospered, nourished by his light.

The word 'star' also referred to the fact that so many theatre luminaries were present that the event had been called the 'Galaxy Ball'.

I have related ad nauseam AMDA's abiding financial troubles, but there were plenty of human ones too. Every semester I had a private session with every student, and some of them wanted to talk about personal problems that had nothing to do with AMDA or their prospective career. I hope I was able to help them, and sometimes I did so when I thought I hadn't; a sympathetic ear can do much. I vividly remember one talented young man to whom I listened compassionately, though I felt he was beyond any help I could give him; later his father came from out of town to thank me for what I had done for his son, and that father was a practising psychiatrist! On another occasion I had to deal with a promising student who had failed in an attempted suicide. More than once I found that the absences of some girl students had been due to their having abortions.

Sometimes there was a problem that affected the whole school. Thus, one year some students came to tell me that another student, whom they wouldn't name, was selling drugs in the school. I made further inquiries and found this to be true. I called the whole school together and told them what I knew. Then I appealed directly to the seller, whom I assumed to be in my audience. I told him that the future of the Academy was in his hands; if he continued to sell drugs at AMDA I would close it. I made it quite clear that I meant what I said and there was great consternation. A few days later the culprit asked to see me; I would never have suspected him. He said it was the only way he knew to pay his school fees and his living costs, and still have time to study. I helped him to get an evening job in a restaurant, and I heard no more about drugs.

The day after the Galaxy Ball I heard that Dial Press had turned down *The Layman*, but I wasn't unduly perturbed because I had had such fun in writing the novel. There followed four other rejections; by that time I should have been surprised by an acceptance. After this I was introduced to a well-known literary agent, James O. Brown, who was to become a good friend of mine. I had already decided on my next project, a novel about William Shakespeare and his youngest brother, Edmund. While absorbed in extensive preparatory study, I was much encouraged by hearing from Bill Decker of the very laudatory reactions he was getting to *The Sole Voice* from notable people to whom he had sent pre-publication copies.

In early July I went to Key West to look at an apartment belonging to a wealthy friend of mine, 'Fritz' Byers. With me went another friend, Charlie Newman, and David Christian, the artist and husband of Katherine Helmond. David was to undertake the renovation to suit my needs. We drove down in a luxurious Cadillac belonging to Fritz. The apartment, which was very near Fritz's house, was potentially perfect for me, and David would remove that modifying adverb, 'potentially'. Fritz and I easily came to terms; I insisted on paying a correct rent but agreed that it should be set against the expenses I would incur in renovating the place.

I had had no contact with Richard since my disappointment at his non-appearance at the Galaxy Ball, but when Aaron told me that on 13 June he would receive the honour of the CBE from the Queen, I immediately sent him a cable of congratulation. It filled my thoughts with what might have happened if he had not moved to Switzerland. Laurence Olivier, now Lord Olivier, the first actor ever to have been so honoured, had once tried to groom Richard to succeed him as Director of the National Theatre, but at the same time, without meaning to, he had discouraged him by complaining about his own difficulties with the Board of Directors, and I feel sure he was more accommodating than Richard would have been. Anyway, Richard had unfortunately become too committed to the values symbolized by the move to Switzerland.

Richard and Elizabeth came to New York briefly in early August, on their way home to Europe. I saw them a few times and went to see them off on the *QE2*. Our meetings were cordial but, for me, disappointing. The trouble over the Galaxy Ball still hung in the air. Richard had been angered by a letter Joyce Worsley had written to him; I had not seen it.

In late August I began to write my novel about William and Edmund Shakespeare, and it became so obsessive that I resented being taken from it by my many engagements. My original title, the loss of which I still regret, was *A Forenoon Knell*. It was taken from an entry in the records of St Saviour's Church, now Southwark Cathedral, on the south bank of the Thames in London. The entry reads, 'Edmund Shakespeare, a player, buried in the Church, with a forenoone knell of the great bell.' To me, a forenoon knell signifies the death of a young man, and Edmund was twenty-seven when he died. I was surprised – and still can't quite believe it – when the publishers, Random House, told me that Americans didn't know the meaning of the word 'knell'. The eventual title was *You, My Brother*. I didn't say so in the book, but it's a quotation from Shakespeare's *Troilus and Cressida*, and is spoken by Troilus in addressing his elder brother, Hector.

Again my busy schedule began to take its toll. I had been

suffering occasional chest pains for some weeks but had ignored them. On 2 September, a year to the day that my angina had been diagnosed, I went to Dial Press to sign some copies of *The Sole Voice* for mailing, and I came away with a heavy parcel of books. The chest pain persisted all day and became so bad by the evening that reluctantly and guiltily I called my doctor at 11 p.m. He told me to get to Lenox Hill Hospital as soon as I could. I then called Al Baruth, who came immediately and took me there. I had had another heart attack.

CHAPTER
Thirteen

The *Today* show announced that I had been taken ill, so the news was soon widespread. Again I was in intensive care and at first I was under heavy sedation. Only near relations are allowed to visit a patient in IC; it was amazing how many near relatives I sprouted during the six days I was there.

Meanwhile *The Sole Voice* was published. This made me eager to get on with *Knell*, as the title appears in my diary, and so I was dismayed to be told, when I had been moved to a beautiful room with a view of Park Avenue, that I would be in the hospital for at least another three weeks. I virtually decided to give up all professional activities except for writing.

Al Baruth tried to persuade me not to move to Key West because he was sure the medical facilities there would be inadequate. How wrong he was! Of course his real motive was a flattering one; he wanted to keep me in New York. But my excellent doctor told me that I shouldn't consider spending any more winters in the north.

When I got home, one of the first things I was legally advised to do was to write a letter resigning from all my remaining activities at AMDA. My doctor had sent a detailed letter to Richard and Elizabeth, and I heard from Aaron's office that they were giving me $3,000 towards my medical and other expenses.

Three weeks after getting out of hospital I left to spend the winter in Key West; in fact I stayed for four and a half months. I was speeded in my departure by a very bad experience, which happened on the first day I took my morning walk on my own. I was going down the steps leading from Riverside Drive to the fountain when, at a turn in these steps invisible from the Drive above and the waterfront below, I found two well-dressed young Blacks waiting for me, one on either side of the steps, apparently lounging. It was Saturday 7 November and I was wearing a winter overcoat. As I passed the inner man he pulled me back against the wall so roughly that the buttons were torn from my coat. In the same instant the other young man had a knife at my throat. I gave them my wallet; they took the money from it, forty dollars, and then surprised me by returning the wallet – I had no credit cards. They quickly disappeared.

My first fear was of another heart attack; nobody happened to come by. As soon as my heart steadied I began very slowly to climb the steps. I was less than ten minutes' walk from my apartment, but it took me well over half an hour to get home. When I had rested awhile I called the police. An officer came quickly and was helpfully sympathetic. I described as well as I could the young men and what they had done. He thought he recognized them – they were a very professional couple – and for some reason he found their giving me back my wallet revealing. If they were caught I would have to go to court to testify. I explained that I would be in Key West and couldn't return during the winter, and that was the last I heard of my assailants.

By a strange coincidence, only a few days before, a friend of mine who was a judge had told me that if ever I was held up, I should tell my attacker(s) that *I* was a judge. I didn't do so because I doubted the wisdom of it. If the assailants were in any way motivated by a sense of social injustice, as so many Blacks had every right to be, to harm a judge might seem a justified act of retribution.

I left for Key West three days after the hold-up, and those three days were filled with friends come to say goodbye and to commiserate over the attack. My apartment had become a bower of flowers, and Al and Charlotte Baruth took all the plants that had to be cared for. I found the journey to Key West a little trying physically, but was pleased to see the apartment gradually being transformed by David Christian into a perfect winter home for me. Richard now wrote me a long letter after a lengthy silence; it made me very happy. As a result of my doctor's letter to him, he strongly approved of the move to Key West.

Before my second heart attack I had been so absorbed in writing *A Forenoon Knell* that I resented anything that took me away from it or from the endless study it involved. I had thought that when I got home from the hospital I should be eager to return to it, but I wasn't. Even in Key West I was slow to take up my work again, and I did so largely from a sense of duty. I had been sure, perhaps because I wanted to believe it, that the local library, unlike the New York Central Library, would be unable to get me the books I needed to consult. There I was surprisingly wrong. The Key West library never failed to obtain the books I requested, even searching as far afield as Harvard University. Early in the new year of 1971 I was busily and happily at work again and *Knell* dominated my first Key West winter.

For my return journey to New York a friend drove me to Miami, and from there I travelled pleasantly by train, arriving on April Fools' Day, an appropriate reminder of a decision I had gradually come to: I would be a fool to live in Manhattan any longer. I was to do no more work at AMDA or in the theatre, and Manhattan was much too demanding a time stealer if I was going to devote myself to writing; moreover, the hold-up was still a vivid memory. While in Key West I had made some tentative inquiries about possible places to live during the summer; at that time a prime condition was easy access to New York. My decision to leave Manhattan for a quieter place and a quieter life soon received a distressing additional justification.

I had gone to see my doctor as soon as I could after my return. He had taken a cardiogram and had been so surprised by it that he thought he should show it to the cardiologist whose patient I had been in the Lenox Hill Hospital. That specialist called me a few days later and said he wanted to see me, but I was not to go to him; he would come to me. A cardiologist making a house visit? That in itself was worrying enough, but what he said when he arrived really scared me. I had suffered new heart damage and had had an 'astonishing escape'. I was to rest completely for a week, not even writing letters, and take a pill every six hours. Then I must see him again after my doctor had carried out more tests. The cardiologist and I had become good friends in the hospital and, after giving me the professional report, he spoke to me informally. From then on I had to lead a very quiet life; if I did, I had a good chance of living another five years. As I write this, that was twenty years ago, and my life hasn't been really quiet. But I obeyed his immediate instructions and set out to enjoy my week of complete rest; I even became grateful for television.

At the end of the week I went to see my doctor. He took lots of tests and told me I had to continue my life of idleness until I heard from the cardiologist. Some time passed and he failed to contact me, so I complained to Aaron who, as always, got things moving. I never heard from the cardiologist again, but my doctor called me. Although he didn't tell me so outright, I sensed that he didn't think my condition was as bad as I had been informed. I immediately went out for a short walk and enjoyed it. My diary reads, 'The trees in the Park are bursting into green. Life is good again.' Soon the days were, as before, too short for me to do all I wanted to do. About this time a belated Easter gift arrived from Richard and Elizabeth which was most inappropriate: a case of liquor. Something must have gone wrong; they knew that I restricted myself to two glasses of wine a day.

One of my friends from the world of show business, Charles Abramson, had been doing a deal of scouting around, chiefly in New Jersey, and had found a place for me to move to from Manhattan. It was a fifth-floor apartment in a large building in Asbury Park, near the boardwalk. Then came the preparations for the move. A few representatives from various companies came to look at my furnishings and give me an estimate. One, who didn't get the job but did get my sympathy, poured out his marital troubles: his wife had run off with his best friend, a priest!

I found myself reluctant to bid a final farewell to AMDA. I

decided not to go to the graduation ceremony but did go to a benefit luncheon only to find that I shouldn't have done so; the emotional experience took its toll of my damaged heart. By this time Christian was well embarked on his spiritual pilgrimage. He was in an ashram in upstate New York. Strangely enough, it was there he began to find his way into the Roman Catholic Church, because many of the people who came there on retreats were priests and nuns wanting to learn the yoga way of meditation.

My first summer in Asbury Park completely justified the move. The long boardwalk by the sea was ideal for my daily exercise; I did much satisfying work on *Knell*; and, to my surprise, there was scarcely a day when I didn't have visitors, some even from Key West. All approved of my apartment, particularly the terrace. I had not seen Christian since he had helped me move into my new home that June, but he came back to pack my things and take me down in a rented car to Key West for the winter.

Richard and Elizabeth had spent the summer in Mexico, where they made an inferior film, *Hammersmith Is Out*. According to the press, Richard was drunk most of the time. I could fully understand that; when he didn't respect the work he was doing, he would seek some relief in alcohol, but it would be controlled by respect for Elizabeth. A few 'friends' in Key West missed no opportunity to show me newspaper cuttings about his drinking, and more than one presented me with a headline from the *New York Times*: 'Whatever Became of Richard Burton?' I was infinitely relieved to get a call from Aaron assuring me that the press accounts were absurdly exaggerated; he even used the phrase 'complete lies'.

For Christmas Richard and Elizabeth were at Elizabeth's home in Gstaad, Switzerland. As my seasonal gifts I sent them some beautiful clothes made by Key West Hand-Print Fabrics. This prompted a front-page article in the local daily newspaper! But the gifts were not delivered by Christmas – in fact, they never arrived. In February I had a delightful but puzzling letter from Elizabeth, full of praise for some kaftans she had received from Budapest. Did she think that was my Christmas gift?

Soon after this, Richard had to deal with a sad bereavement. Ivor, his favourite brother and constant companion, died, having been an invalid for three and a half years as the result of a fall.

My main objective while in Key West was to finish *Knell*. It wasn't easy because winter there is the social season; but, in spite of all the pleasant distractions, I did finish the book on 17 March 1972. It had been such an intimate part of my life for so long that I felt at a loss without it. Its inordinate size was going to be a problem in getting it published; it contained well over 400,000 words.

When the time came to leave Key West, I easily settled down again in Asbury Park, though I felt lost without *Knell* – I always feel guilty if I'm not working on something. In early June came the news from my agent that Random House would publish *Knell* provided I cut it by at least a quarter; even then it would be a large book of 300,000 words. Reluctantly I agreed to the terms and set to work at once. It was a very difficult task, and I grieved at some of the excisions I had to make – it was like losing friends who had meant much to me. At the same time, by way of consolation, the idea for my next book occurred to me: a fictional autobiography of General John Burgoyne, 'Gentleman Johnny', who had first caught my interest fifty years before in Bernard Shaw's *The Devil's Disciple*. A few days later it struck me how timely the work would be with the bicentennial celebration coming up in 1976.

In the midst of all this work I had the shock of hearing that my friend Fritz Byers had been found drowned in his pool. By a tragically ironic coincidence, on the day after I heard the news came two letters from Fritz, one of them heartbreakingly happy. I felt I had to go to the funeral, though I was urgently busy, but I was persuaded not to.

A very delayed Christmas letter from Richard now disturbed me still further. He had written it on Christmas Eve, but I didn't get it until 16 June. I had received his Christmas gift long before, but that had come through Aaron. Some of the letter had been left out of the envelope; I couldn't decide whether this had been done deliberately or from carelessness. The disturbing news was that a test had revealed that his liver was enlarged, probably from too much alcohol. I longed to be with him.

In Asbury Park I had started work on a modern novel. I decided that I wanted to try something needing no research, so *Gentleman Johnny* would have to wait. One day when my agent, James Brown, was sharing a walk with me, he suggested that with my analytical mind I ought to try my hand at a mystery novel. A few days later an idea occurred to me and I started work at once. Now in Key West, with *Knell* out of the way, it dominated my life, and I was writing about 2,000 words a day – but I had set myself a limit of 100,000 words this time! It was entitled *My Friend, the Enemy*, but the trouble with the story was that the characters took such possession of me that the murder simply would not take place. Would the characters have the same appeal to the readers? I could only hope so. There was a death, but it was the result of an accident in which the character I had intended to be the murderer was involved. The theme was the clash of values between two generations, typified by a father and daughter.

In February 1973 I had my first examination by a doctor new to Key West, Robert Carraway, and I gained such confidence in him as a physician, and such admiration of him as a man, both of which have never been shaken, that for the first time I began to think of making Key West my permanent home. However, I was in no hurry to do so, and that summer I returned once more to Asbury Park, where I spent my time reading in preparation for my book on Burgoyne, and entertaining numerous most welcome guests, until a day in late June. Aaron phoned to tell me the surprising news that Richard and Elizabeth were staying with him at his summer home in Quogue, Long Island, and in a later call he made it clear that he would be glad when they left. Then I got a long call from Elizabeth, who was very worried about Richard; he was in a bad mood and drinking heavily. That same day I was awakened by the telephone just before midnight: it was Richard. He was obviously drunk. He said he had been asked to review my novel *Knell*, or *You, My Brother* as it was now to be called. He thought it was for *The New Yorker*. He said he would come to see me. The following day I found that my editor at Random House, Charlotte Mayerson, was happy about the possible review by Richard and had sent a copy of the galleys of the book to Aaron's office. That was the last I heard about the review.

A week passed with no further word from or about Richard and Elizabeth, and then a friend, who was in hospital in New York recovering from an operation, called to read me a headline in the *Daily News*: Richard and Elizabeth were separating! I called Aaron. He told me that the marriage was becoming a mess, and that the camera ghouls were out in force in Quogue. Perhaps it was good for me at this time that I had an unbroken succession of visitors.

It was ironic that my next call to Aaron was to wish him a happy birthday. There were three birthdays in the Frosch family close together, so I usually sent one parcel containing three gifts. Aaron's wife Bobby called to thank me, and gave me a horrendous account of the past few weeks. All the while, whenever visitors allowed me the time, I was dutifully trying to study material for the Burgoyne book, but I wasn't succeeding very well, and I spent hours watching the television coverage of Watergate.

One evening I received a long call from Aaron, whose sole purpose was to cheer me up; he also suggested I should write to Richard. I did so at once, and felt better for it. Then on 1 August came the news on the *Today* show that Richard and Elizabeth were planning a divorce. I felt very frustrated at not hearing from either of them, and a few days later I wrote to Elizabeth. Aaron had kept in frequent touch with me, so it was a great surprise to hear, not from him but on the radio, that he and Bobby had gone to Italy. The information proved to be false; it was Richard and Elizabeth who had left. The marriage was a seesaw; they could no longer live together or live apart.

Then I heard that a film Richard had gone to make had been postponed, and he was coming back to New York, alone. I ached to see him, but was cheered to read the first notice of *You, My Brother* in late August; this review was in *Publishers' Weekly* and was one of unstinted praise. The novel was to be published in the fall, and the English publication would take place the following March.

Disappointed at not having heard from Richard, I called Aaron and was surprised to learn that Richard was again in Quogue. He was under a doctor's care because he had sciatica and a painful leg. Richard said that, as soon as he was well enough, he would come down to see me. We did not mention Elizabeth. I called him a few days later but there was no reply. From Aaron I learned that Richard was in the Regency Hotel, so I called him there and said I was looking forward to his visit. He phoned back a few days later, but to tell me of his latest dilemma resulting from a personal involvement with Sophia Loren; he might shortly be leaving for Rome. The following day I heard from Aaron, who said that Richard was exaggerating his dilemma. That was on a Saturday. On the Monday Richard called; he was not going to Rome – instead, he was coming to see me the following day. But he didn't come; the doctor said he shouldn't travel because he had intestinal flu. On the Friday I went to New York, and the doctor reassured me about Richard. He certainly looked well but had some difficulty in walking. Still, he decided to come back to Asbury Park with me and stay until the Sunday evening.

There followed a wonderful weekend in which we made up for years of much-needed conversation. I think it helped him; I was told later that he was 'a different man' afterwards. Although it was painful for him to walk, he insisted on coming out with me a few times. On one of our excursions we were sitting on a bench at the unfrequented end of the boardwalk when a small group of teenage boys came by. One of them recognized Richard and, very tentatively, came over to speak to him. When he was told that he was indeed speaking to Richard Burton he became starry-eyed and stammered. Richard dealt with him delightfully and ended by giving him a twenty-dollar bill. When the boy had gone with his friends, all of them repeatedly looking back, Richard said with a smile, 'His mother will never believe it, and as for the twenty dollars. . . !'

The news of Richard's being in Asbury Park soon spread, and we were spied on whenever we took our little walks. On the Saturday we called Elizabeth, who was in Rome. It was not an easy conversation and got nowhere. I felt the situation was hopeless. My sympathy was with her when Richard left me on the Sunday evening, because in the car which came to fetch him was a pleasant and pretty young actress. I felt protective towards her, too, because she was so vulnerable. But, in spite of all, it had been a very worthwhile weekend. I was not surprised to hear on the following Wednesday that Richard had flown to Montana for solitude, but he was soon back in New York on his way to Italy. I went to see him, but failed to speak with him alone. I felt his condition had deteriorated, both physically and psychologically, and I was depressed by this. I longed to have a private hour with him, but it was not to be. The next I heard from Aaron was that Richard was again in Quogue, and with him was another young woman, not the one I had met in Asbury Park.

During our weekend together Richard and I had had a preliminary discussion on a subject that was to occupy us for years, and only his untimely death was to prevent it from coming to fruition. It was to do a play about Shakespeare's Richard III as he appears not only in the play of that name but also in *Henry VI, Parts 2 and 3*, where he is the Duke of Gloucester. His best and most revealing soliloquy is in *Henry VI, Part 3*. I was by no means the first to think of this. Colley Cibber had had the same idea in the year 1700, and his version had held the stage for more than a century; however, there's as much Cibber as Shakespeare in it – Shakespeare's text was not as sacrosanct then as it is now. I wanted to work out a version that was wholly Shakespeare's. Most ironically, eleven years later in my last phone conversation with Richard, who was in Europe, he talked about the project and of how much he looked forward to coming to Key West early in the new year, when he would stay with me for a month to work on the new *Richard III* and *King Lear*.

Two weeks after Richard had left me there was a pleasantly unexpected postscript to his visit. He was usually very remiss in polite correspondence, but he sent signed photographs and appreciative handwritten letters to an Asbury Park doctor who had helped him, and to friends of mine, whose apartment he had visited. Much more characteristically, he also sent signed photographs to my cleaning woman and the doorman.

After months of study I finally settled down to writing the novel now entitled *They Called Me Gentleman Johnny*, which I had decided to do in the form of an autobiography. Few people realize that Burgoyne was a good writer. A play of his, *The Heiress*, was considered by some contemporaries to be better than any of Sheridan's. Many Americans, when in London, go to see the equestrian statue of General Burgoyne, assuming it to be the man who lost the battle of Saratoga, thus assuring the establishment of the USA. That statue is indeed that of a General John Burgoyne, but he was the illegitimate son of Gentleman Johnny. The more I learned about the elder Burgoyne, who was born in 1722, the more fascinating did he become to me. I tried to capture the style of eighteenth-century English in the opening words of a foreword I had him write: 'Old age is a plaguey affliction.'

They Called Me Gentleman Johnny dominated my work that season in Key West, and it was virtually finished by the time I left on 30 April. While I was working on it I received a great disappointment: my agent, Jim Brown, had failed to sell the murder mystery, *My Friend, the Enemy*. I had felt it would be readily saleable; I was much more dubious about my Burgoyne book because its style would limit its appeal, but I counted on the bicentennial celebration in 1976 to arouse interest. *You, My Brother* was published in London, and in connection with that I gave some interviews by transatlantic phone. The interviewers were generally more interested in talking about Richard than about my book, but I studiously disappointed them. *You, My Brother* was also published in paperback editions, both in the USA and England. The American edition gave me a welcome opportunity to correct errors that had escaped me in the original book, but the English edition, which was published by what I was told was a prestigious paperback house, was an incredible absurdity. I had been asked if I would allow an anglicization of the spelling. I welcomed the idea, assuming I would make the changes myself. I heard no more; then I saw the book in print. Here is an extract from a letter I wrote to accompany a four-page list of serious errors:

> Of course, most of the errors are due to carelessness, but the origin of some of them is beyond my understanding; for example, 'Sunday' has become 'Saturday', 'stench' – 'strength', 'unchastened' – 'unchristened', and 'Physician' – 'Providence'. While I am happy to see the spelling made British for British readers, there are some strange lapses. Thus, 'stupour' doesn't exist in any dictionary on either side of the Atlantic.

Another activity which occupied much of my time in the '73–'74 season, apart from the usual demands of visitors and visiting, was the search for a permanent home. I had definitely decided that I would spend the rest of my life in Key West. Two homes were an unnecessary expense, and there was the trouble twice a year of finding a driver to take me from one to the other. (I don't drive; I don't even ride a bicycle.) As to which of my places of residence, north or south, should be the one in which to spend my last years, my heart condition decided that. With helpful friends I examined several houses, apartments and condominiums; something was wrong with all of them. I wanted to avoid stairs; I didn't want anyone living above me (my experience in my last New York apartment had taught me that lesson), or too much expense; and I wanted necessary places such as stores, the bank and a post office to be within walking distance. I left without finding what I wanted.

As soon as I got back to Asbury Park I called Aaron to get news of Richard; I was relieved to hear he was in a hospital, 'drying out', but not so happy to hear that it looked as though the divorce was going ahead. I had written to the manager of my

Asbury Park apartment building to inform him that I should be leaving permanently in November, and the news had got out. People I didn't know mentioned it with flattering sadness.

It was a month before I went to Manhattan. I was beginning to find that I resented all travel, and this was, perhaps subconsciously, another reason for settling in one place. In Manhattan I went to the office of the SSDC to resign as Honorary Advisor, but they wouldn't hear of it. I also visited several friends, but particularly Aaron. He had a dismal report on Richard, but I was even more dismayed by his own condition. He had been found to have a rare kind of multiple sclerosis, and had sadly deteriorated. It's a particularly cruel disease because the mind remains acutely aware of increasing physical disability, which can go on for years and years. I had watched it happen to a friend of mine in Wales, and it was agony to watch Aaron, too, slowly decay to a merciful death.

On 6 June came a very exciting call from Christian, who was spending the summer in Key West; he had found what could be made into a perfect home for me. How right he was! His judgement in such matters is infinitely better than mine, and I readily agreed to buy it, sight-unseen. I found later from the documents that the main part of the house had been built in 1890. It was being offered at a bargain price but was apparently in a run-down condition. When it was known that I intended to buy the property I received some letters from Key West friends advising me against it, but they were wrong and Christian was right; they saw what was but he saw what might be. There was a widespread feeling in Key West, I suppose from my association with Richard, that I was an eccentric millionaire – eccentric, maybe – so by the time the realtor spoke to me, the original price had gone up thirty per cent. It was still a bargain, and remained so even though it cost twice as much again to renovate. When the news of my buying the house was published in the local press, the estimates Christian had received from contractors all went up as well. Five months' work by carpenters, plumbers and electricians had been done on the house before I saw it, and another three months elapsed before I moved in.

Even after that Christian himself kept working on it for another year.

Before the end of June I received a longed-for and reassuring call from Richard. He was in New York but was leaving the following day for Europe. He sounded in good form and made me very happy by saying he wanted to return to the stage; in particular he wanted me to make a cut version of Sartre's *Le Diable et le Bon Dieu*. (Like *The Beach of Falesá*, the film script of *Coriolanus*, and other projects he would ask me to work on for him, it would never see production.) He told me the divorce was definitely going through, even though Elizabeth was trying to stop it. I told him about the house in Key West, and he said that someday he would visit me there; that was a promise he did keep.

I had finished the Burgoyne book and sent it to my agent. While I eagerly awaited the reaction to it, I felt lost without the daily work, so more than ever did I welcome visiting friends, of which there was an abundance since that would be my last summer in Asbury Park. They included my niece, Megan, who came from Wales for two weeks. Aaron insisted on my having a farewell weekend with the family at Quogue, and it was the best ever. His three daughters, Juliana, Phoebe and Suzanna, were all there. I had known them all their lives, and we had enjoyed Sunday afternoon walks together in the Park when they were children. They had grown beautifully. Juliana had come home from college for the special weekend. I enjoyed helping Phoebe fill out her application for Wellesley, and then she took me for a ride in her jeep.

I made other goodbye visits to Manhattan, including one to AMDA. Financial troubles persisted, but so did the school. My visit there – certainly my last one, but I tried not to think of that – was a happy one, except that I was disappointed that Joyce Worsley was going to resign in the new year; she had chosen her successor from the staff, and I approved of her choice.

Christian came up to help me with my packing for the last move in my life. He did it all, except for books and manuscripts; those were my responsibility, all fifty cartons of them. On

Wednesday 13 November the movers came at 8.30 a.m. and were away by 1 p.m. Christian and I left in a rented car an hour later. It was the end of a fruitful association with New York that had lasted since I first settled there, twenty years before.

CHAPTER
Fourteen

When we got to Key West the first thing I had to do was see my new home. I'm sure it was a nerve-racking moment for Christian, but I was wholly taken with the sight of the house, even in its unfinished state. Christian was going to stay there but I would be in the apartment for another three months. My seventieth-birthday celebrations took place soon afterwards, and they were truly memorable. Christian prepared my first meal in the new house, and our friend and neighbour Gary Heimann threw a champagne party. It was extraordinary to find how many friends I had in my new home town.

A few days after my birthday came a long letter from Richard, mailed from Rome and sent c/o Aaron. Strangely enough I still possess that letter; strangely, because I have what some of my friends think is a ridiculous conscience in this matter. To me, a private letter is intended only for the eyes of the person to whom it is addressed, and as soon as I have replied to one I destroy it. But now even I regret having destroyed some, especially those from distinguished authors. How I came to preserve four from Richard I don't know, but I'm very glad I did. They don't even belong together because they range in date from 1956 to 1979. Two of them are from the year 1974: a birthday letter dated 21 November and another dated 3 November. Both were written, or rather typed, on the stationery of Le Grand Hotel, Rome, and had much to say about the rumours circulating in the press concerning his imminent marriage to Princess Elisabeth of Yugoslavia. Again my conscience won't let me share his confidences in that matter with my reader, but a few things I can share. I was very relieved to read, 'I am as boozeless as a Mother Superior and as industrious as an army ant.' He had taken 'Princess Zablac' for a motoring vacation in Morocco:

> There I hired a Hertz self-drive Renault, low in power but high in anonymity, and drove all over the place. We frequented the Souks and Casbahs unguided, which we were told later was a perilous thing to do. However, I can only assume that my fame protected us, for everybody, young and old, seemed to know me. I was called variously by solemn jellabaed old wizened men, probably no older than I am, Saint Becket or Major Smith. The latter puzzled me for a time until I discovered from John Huston, whom we found casually in the middle of the Atlas Mountains, that *Where Eagles Dare* had been a huge success in Morocco and had been playing for months, while *Becket* seems to be a perennial.

Richard had been elected a Fellow of his Oxford college and, as such, was expected to go there to give some lectures. He asked my help. 'I want to talk about the corruption of power and success. I have been very aware of this in my own case and have, as a result of playing Churchill, become more and more obsessed by it. The pathology of leadership is one very near my heart.' As for the Princess, there was a report in the Christmas number of *Time* that she had left Richard because he had resumed his drinking, and this proved to be true.

After a happy Christmas with numerous friends, local and visiting, I settled down to writing a new book, a novel about the Elizabethan poet and playwright Christopher Marlowe. I have a firm belief that he was murdered. The official account of his death was that it had been an accident resulting from a gambling quarrel. A line in Shakespeare's *As You Like It*, which has puzzled many scholars, seems to me to refer clearly to this: '... it strikes a man more dead than a great reckoning in a little room.' Marlowe's death was certainly in Shakespeare's mind when he wrote *As You Like It*, for in it he quotes from Marlowe's unfinished poem *Hero and Leander*:

> Dead shepherd, now I find thy saw of might,
> Whoever loved that loved not at first sight?

The only two witnesses to Marlowe's death were the two men who I believe were his paid murderers. Even before I had written a word of the book I knew its title: *A Great Reckoning*. A rejection by the publishers Houghton Mifflin of my book on Burgoyne had said it was 'not exciting enough for fiction, not factual enough for history'. I was determined my Marlowe book should be exciting enough. I wrote to Jim Brown to tell him to give up his efforts to sell *They Called Me Gentleman Johnny*, which had had seven rejections; a friend reminded me that *Gone with the Wind* had had more than three times that number. I worked feverishly on *A Great Reckoning* and finished it by mid-July, but was utterly dismayed when Jim Brown said it wasn't commercial enough to submit to any publisher. The news paralysed my pen for some years.

The surprise of that year was that Richard and Elizabeth were together again, and had actually remarried, this time in Africa. When I received their joint Christmas present, again added to by Aaron, it seemed as if all was as it had been, but when I recalled Richard's letters and what he had told me, I had grave doubts about their future together.

Another surprise was also a great relief. Hanging over me for more than ten years had been the threat of having to pay a large and growing amount of tax, now well over $25,000, incurred by AMDA when it was a commercial enterprise, before it became my responsibility. My supposed obligation was now finally cancelled as the result of Aaron's untiring efforts.

Early in 1976 Richard and Elizabeth were in New York, but things were not going well with them. There was a new reason for that: Susan Hunt, who was also in New York. Richard had met her in Switzerland. His second divorce from Elizabeth was inevitable. He went to Haiti to obtain it, and in August, in Arlington, Virginia, Susan became the third Mrs Richard

Burton. There was a happy side to the news: Richard was off the booze again, and was making a successful return to the Broadway stage in *Equus*. When he had settled down in the play he very much wanted me to see his Dysart, but I had made a vow to myself that I would never travel any long distance again, and I have kept it.

But one part of my former life I did resume: I decided to give some lectures, this time for the benefit of my church, St Paul's Episcopal. I revived two of my old lectures: *The Miracle That Was Shakespeare* and *Comedy through the Ages*. I had never used a script or even notes, and this meant relearning many hundreds of lines from plays. I was relieved to find that this was still comparatively easy, and both evenings were highly successful.

Soon after Richard had married Susan he called me from a hotel in New York in order to introduce me to her over the phone. We both meant it when we said we were longing to meet each other, and Richard promised they would come for a visit as soon as he was free. He was so busy making films, good and bad, that it was a year before he was able to do so. In September 1977 he and Susan arrived for a five-day visit. I was worried that I wouldn't be able to ensure their privacy in such an intimate place as Key West, where it would be impossible to prevent the news of their arrival from spreading quickly. Susan would be free to roam around, but would Richard have to be a prisoner in the house? All worked out well, however. Only twice did the three of us venture out together, to St Paul's Church on Sunday morning, and to a restaurant. At the latter place we were seated in a private corner with Gary Heimann, but were found by a friend with a worrisome camera.

I had planned some special meals only to discover that Richard and Susan wanted very plain food and very little of that, but it was good to see Richard in one of his 'dry' spells; he would not touch even a glass of wine. Susan loyally followed him in his choices of food and drink. As the news spread of their being in town there was usually a small group outside the house waiting to get a glimpse of Richard, and some of them succeeded because every afternoon Gary came to take him to his house to enjoy a swim in his pool, protected by a wall from prying eyes. It was Gary who had taken me to meet them at the airport. To avoid the small public planes from Miami they had arrived in a private Lear jet. I immediately approved of Susan, and my instinctive liking for her increased during their stay. But then, I heartily approved of all four wives once I got to know them. Susan was destined to have the hardest time with Richard, because she virtually had to become his nurse during a long illness, and he was a very difficult patient.

Richard spent much of the time reading, a habit of long standing. He was eager to read my Burgoyne 'autobiography', and he genuinely enjoyed it. Then he wanted to hear the recording of a lecture I had recently given on *Hamlet*; he smiled as he listened to it because it brought back many memories. On their third night Susan stayed up after Richard went to bed. She wanted a long talk with me and I was grateful for it. When Richard went to swim in Gary's pool, we enjoyed going on shopping expeditions together.

What did Richard and I talk about? We relived the past, we talked about Kate, whose twentieth birthday would be two days after they left, and, of course, we talked Shakespeare. He became excited about my ideas for the new version of *Richard III*, but chiefly he wanted me to talk about *King Lear*. He had an increasing desire to play the title role, which thrilled me.

I didn't keep Richard and Susan entirely to myself. The Rector of St Paul's, Eric Potter, now a canon at St Andrew's Cathedral in Honolulu, usually came back to breakfast with me after Mass on Tuesdays, and he did so while Richard and Susan were here. On that occasion Richard spoke fascinatingly about Marshal Tito, whom he had met and stayed with when he had gone to Yugoslavia to make the government-sponsored film *The Battle of Sutjeska*, in which he played Tito. The President and the actor had got on very well together, and Richard had come away filled with admiration for Tito.

I also gave an afternoon sherry party so that some of my friends could meet my visitors. There were ten guests. In the light of all the publicity about Richard's drinking, they must have been impressed by the fact that he confined himself to Perrier water. It was a very pleasant afternoon. One of the guests was my doctor, Robert Carraway, and I noticed that Richard found an opportunity to take him aside; I assume the subject of their conversation was my health.

The last morning was spent at Gary's house and we had lunch there before he took us to the airport. When I got back I found five $100 bills in the study. I was both touched and hurt. Why hurt? I had always gratefully accepted gifts of money for my birthday and Christmas, but this was different, almost like an elaborate tip.

When Richard called me from London on my birthday, he asked me several questions about *King Lear*. I promised to write a long letter to answer them and did so the next day. I was very happy to know that he had been giving serious study to the text.

At Christmas I received a gift from Richard and Susan – and one from Elizabeth.

CHAPTER
Fifteen

On 14 February 1978 I delivered a lecture on *Macbeth*, the proceeds of which went once again to my parish church, St Paul's. Perhaps my chief impulse in interpreting *Macbeth* was to restore what I considered to be Shakespeare's conception of the relationship between Macbeth and his Lady. Ever since Sarah Siddons made theatrical history in the eighteenth century with her playing of Lady Macbeth, there has been a tendency to make her the dominant character in the play. This could not have been Shakespeare's intention. The first Lady Macbeth was played by a boy, and no boy could have dominated the first Macbeth, Richard Burbage. Shakespeare didn't even give her a name; she was just an adjunct to Macbeth. To me she is a woman, not a monster. Those who see her as the epitome of evil are reduced to saying that her very human fainting was feigned, but Shakespeare gives no indication of that.

To my relief the lecture-recital was one of my greatest successes as a performer, judging from the subsequent comments I received or heard about; my diary records it as having had 'an extraordinary impact'. My one regret was that Richard had not heard it. If he had, he might have been persuaded to play Macbeth. He had not shown any interest in doing so; but then, I had had to persuade him to play Coriolanus, and that had, perhaps, been his greatest role.

On 5 March I had my longest phone conversation ever with Richard. His call came from New York and lasted two and a quarter hours; it was all about *King Lear*. It seemed that a

Broadway production was in preparation, but already difficulties had arisen which resulted in the replacement of the English director John Dexter by an American, Elia Kazan. The chief object of the phone conversation was to decide on the maximum cuts in the text that could be made, as Richard wanted to be fully armed for any discussions that might take place with the director. He had already committed the whole of the part to memory, but further difficulties arose and the production was unhappily abandoned while still at the planning stage. *King Lear* was so much on my mind that I decided it should be the subject of my next lecture-recital for the benefit of St Paul's Church.

I had a rather embarrassing experience in November of that year. Paul Ferris, a writer originally from Wales but now based in London, had contacted me earlier to get Richard's co-operation for a biography that he was writing. The previous year he had published a biography of Dylan Thomas. (Incidentally, in 1985 he admirably edited a collection of Dylan's letters.) I had expected that Richard's response would be negative, but I was surprised by how strongly negative it was; the reason for this was his angry reaction to the biography of Dylan, in which the poet's work, which is all that really matters to the world, is overshadowed by an account of the seamier side of his life. I wonder what Richard would have said about some of the biographies that later appeared about himself. Fortunately, I am convinced that he could never have been induced to read them. I had to make it quite clear to Paul Ferris that Richard would not see him, speak to him, or write to him.

Paul had written to me not only because of my relation to Richard but because he had known me personally. It must have been about thirty years previously, when he was still in Wales and starting out as a writer. He had submitted a script to me at the BBC in Cardiff, and I had accepted it, thus helping to launch him in his career. He had found our relationship at that time pleasant and helpful. Having failed to contact Richard, he wanted to come to Key West to talk to me about him. He was the first of three biographers who have sought my co-operation. I have firmly refused it. If our story was to be told, it would have to be told in my words; hence, at long last, this book.

Then, in October, Paul Ferris received a commission from the BBC to do a thirty-minute edited interview with me for radio, the subject being Philip Burton, not Richard. I made it quite clear by telephone and letter, and also when we met, that I would not speak about Richard except in the most general terms. Paul arrived on the 21st and left on 25 November. On a personal level his visit was a very amicable one, during which I took him to a Thanksgiving Day dinner at the home of a dear friend of mine. As for the interviews, we had four long sessions, resulting in hours of recordings. In spite of my preliminary caution, Paul persisted in questioning me about Richard. I liked Paul and was torn between a desire to help him and the knowledge of Richard's absolute refusal to do so. I was careful to say little about Richard, and nothing that he or his loved ones could object to, but I was left with the feeling that the whole project had been a ruse to get something private out of me about him. On the other hand, I had to admit that a programme about me had to include something about Richard. In the final editing, reducing hours of tapes down to half an hour, not a single reference to Richard had been omitted. Even after he returned home, Paul sent me a few letters with probing questions about Richard. Finally I had to write a stern letter which stopped our correspondence.

In February 1979 the lecture-recital on *King Lear* took place. It had become a big event, with people travelling long distances for it. Undoubtedly it was the single most demanding experience of my professional career – and in my seventy-fifth year! Afterwards, I decided that I would never again undertake such a colossal task; lectures perhaps, but not lecture-recitals, especially on such a gigantic subject. As if the play itself were not a sufficient challenge, things went wrong from the beginning. Ten minutes before I was due to start, a man in the audience had a heart attack; an ambulance was called and he was taken to hospital. In addition, I was told later, the sound system had not worked. Had I known that I would not have gone on, because the acoustics of the large hall were bad. In spite of all, the nearly two-hour-long ordeal was worth it; I achieved a notable success, both for myself and for St Paul's Church. There was one last mishap. My chief reason for choosing *King Lear* as my subject was Richard's great desire to play the part, and I looked forward to sending him a tape of the evening; but the recording machine broke down!

My next engagement, on Friday 13 April, was most unexpected and deeply meaningful. It was Good Friday. At the invitation and in the presence of my Bishop, James Duncan, I gave addresses from the pulpit of St Paul's Church on 'The Seven Last Words of Christ'. I wore a black cassock. The preparation of the addresses, which I wrote out in full, helped me to examine my faith, and I was deeply gratified in the following days by comments I received from strangers who had attended the service.

I had little contact with Richard and Susan except for an occasional letter, and gifts for my birthday and Christmas. Frequently I didn't know where they were. Often I would feel grieved by the silence, and then would come a letter to soothe the hurt. One such letter, a six-page handwritten one, came for my birthday in November, and I later found it with the few that somehow evaded the fate of most of the letters I received. Here are some extracts from it, one of which I blush to include but do so because the reader may find it amusing:

> Just arrived here, in Los Angeles, after a very uncomfortable 10 weeks or so in Toronto, where I did a film called *Circle of Two*. Director: Jules Dassin – nice but a bit old-fashioned. Co-star: one Tatum Oneal [*sic*], daughter of Ryan (*Love Story*) Oneal: also nice and moderately talented. She's only 15 and 3/4, so allowances must be made. She may become very good. Hard to tell. The discomfort was occasioned not by them nor the script, which I think is quite good, but by the weather and an incompetent crew.
>
> Enclosed is Rowse's *New Annotated Shakespeare*. He's, as usual, very waspish and sometimes witty, but chiefly I thought you'd be amused by the photographs they've chosen

to accompany the text. Those give us a temporary immortality – until the next one comes out!

We stay here (L'Hermitage Hotel, 9291 Burton Way, Beverly Hills) until my birthday is thankfully over – how I hate anniversaries! – when we will leave for Puerto Vallarta for a few weeks, after which I expect I'll do some film or other (there are a couple of interesting ones) and then in May (I think) I go into rehearsals for *Camelot* again. I shall play it for a year. If that doesn't get me fit for *Lear* nothing will [. . . .]

Word of your enormous success with the latest lecture reached me from all kinds of sources. I smiled modestly and said I'd taught you all you knew! I tell people you don't do anything as common as lecture; that we must coin a new word for what you do to that audience. I tell them that you explode with more passion in one 'lecture' than I do in ten performances of *Hamlet*. What shall we call them? Lectureagonistesappassionata? Impressive on a billboard don't you think?

My eldest brother Tom died, as I think you know, a few weeks ago – no, several weeks ago – nearly making his 79th; not bad with two lungs full of coal. Susan and I went to the funeral. Susan was overwhelmed by the singing; the whole valley was out in force. It was a curious irony that his only child, Mair, who has been married for twenty years, suddenly found herself pregnant *for the first time* at the age of 41. What's more, the baby has arrived, a girl, and mother and child are in splendid order. The Lord giveth. . . .

Cis was at the funeral and angelic as ever. Naturally she sent especial love to you. 'Oh, I wish I 'ad all that's in 'is 'ead.' Imagine if you'd caught that bright loving creature when she was young.

If we get a chance we'll nip in and see you. If not, we'll try and get *Camelot* to Miami.

When is the next lectureagonistesappassionata? Tell those idiots to get the taping right for once, will you?

Am in splendid health (apart from a temporary cold) and Susan too. Cannot, however, give up smoking, whereas booze is a distant (and regretfully delightful) memory. Will try again with the nicotine and tar. Dangerous though, as the last time I gave it up – for five days – I *totally* lost my memory. Apparently it's not at all unusual.

Happy birthday. Much love, and from Susan too. Usual apologies for long silence.

P.S. Kate is at the Yale School of Drama if you want to drop her a line.

Kate. Neither Richard nor I wanted her to become an actress – it can be a heartbreaking profession – but she did follow her father and mother and is doing well. Like her father too, she is an infrequent correspondent, but when we do get in contact it is always a wonderful experience. She and her husband, Michael Ritchie, have not yet found their way to Key West, but I'm confident that they will. They now have a delightful little son, Morgan.

In that letter from Richard greetings were included from two of Elizabeth's children, Christopher Wilding and Maria Burton; her other children weren't there. The story of Maria bears wonderful testimony to Elizabeth's great compassion. She very much wanted to have a child by Richard, but her three children had all been born by Caesarean section, and she had had a very bad time in giving birth to the last, Liza Todd, so the doctors had finally seen to it that she couldn't have any more. She decided to adopt a child, who would be at least legally a Burton. It was in Germany that she found the child. The authorities urged her to take the most perfect baby available for adoption, but Elizabeth chose the one that was most in need of her loving care. The baby girl was nine months old, covered with sores, badly malnourished and with such a crippled hip that she was unlikely ever to be able to walk. She became Maria Burton, and a near miracle happened as a result of medical care, surgery and family love; after two years she began to walk and subsequently she could even run. She has grown into a normal, lovely and loving young woman.

Early in the new year, 1980, Elizabeth got in touch with me. She wanted me to go to Palm Beach, where she was to receive an award. Unfortunately it was an evening affair, and so, much though I wanted to see her again, I had to decline. Two months later she called asking me to go and stay with her and her husband, John Warner, by that time Senator Warner. She was exploring the possibility of a poetry recital with Burt Reynolds, and said she needed my help. Apparently it was to be a more lighthearted affair than the original one with Richard sixteen years before. When I explained why I couldn't visit her, she asked me to send her some suggestions for poems. I did so the next day; in particular I recommended Ogden Nash. A month later I heard from her again, or rather from an intermediary; Elizabeth herself was in hospital and her condition baffled the doctors. This time her request was a truly surprising one; would I dramatize Henry James's *Portrait of a Lady*? Nothing came of it, but it was clear that that experience long ago of a stage and a live audience had left her with a happy memory, and she seemed determined to try the theatre again. She did, and she made sure that I would see her.

I had been much gratified by the success of the Good Friday addresses I had given in St Paul's Church the previous year. The preparation for these had helped me greatly in finding and testing my faith, which had been strong in my youth and early manhood, but had become slack in middle age; now it had returned and was increasingly vital to me. As a result of that initiation in speaking from the pulpit, I had agreed to give six Lenten addresses in 1980, starting on Ash Wednesday. I chose as my subject the Lord's Prayer. It is very hard to bring to full life, when we utter them, words we know so well; we tend to rattle them off meaninglessly.

Another rich experience that year, but of a very different kind, was a visit to Miami by Richard and Susan. Richard was playing in a revival, after twenty years, of *Camelot*. He had been very disappointed that I was unable to see him in *Equus* on Broadway, but he had had to accept that my travelling days were over. However, he was determined that I should see *Camelot*, particularly since I had been so closely connected with the original production, and so he insisted that the post-Broadway tour should include Miami. The production was there for four weeks in October–November.

While the show was in New York I had been bombarded with news, press cuttings and rumours about Richard. Most notable was the publicity that had resulted from his failure to complete the performance on 17 July, when he had had to be replaced by his understudy. With Richard's reputation it was inevitable that many people, perhaps most, assumed that he had been too drunk to continue. The truth was that he was suffering from a pinched nerve in the neck, which would ultimately force him to give up the part completely before the long tour ended. It was only medication that enabled him to go on at all. In spite of his disability he had received excellent notices, some even preferring his performance to the original one in 1960.

The engagement opened in Miami on Monday 20 October. I waited for Richard to tell me when he wanted me to see the show, knowing that it wouldn't be in the first week; he would want time to get used to the theatre. But he was forestalled by a good and generous friend of mine, Mary Spottswood, who without reference to me reserved five seats for the first Saturday matinée and took us up in the family limousine. The other three members of the party were my very dear friend and Mary's mother-in-law, Florence Spottswood, Gary, and the driver, Bill Carlough.

I had not told Richard about our coming because I knew he would have wanted to postpone the visit, but when we got to the theatre I decided it would be unfair not to let him know that I was there. I went to the stage door alone – my friends could see him after the performance – but there was such a strict control on admittance that someone in authority had to be fetched before I was allowed in.

When we got to the dressing room the first thing that struck me was that Susan was doing Richard's make-up; his right arm was virtually useless. On stage he wielded his sword with his left arm. When he had recovered from the surprise of seeing me and I had explained the circumstances, he asked me where we were sitting. I told him we had good seats halfway back. He called the house manager and asked him to change our seats to ones nearer the stage. The house was completely sold out, so how the manager could do this I didn't know, but he did; we had centre seats in about the sixth row.

The script had been skilfully adapted to allow for Richard's added twenty years; it began with a prologue in which King Arthur was middle aged, and then the tale became a reminiscence. I did not have to maintain my usual critical appreciation of the show and of Richard's performance – they weren't on their way to Broadway – so I was free just to relax and enjoy it, and I did.

At the end Richard received a standing and vociferous ovation, and then he made a speech about me which was so deeply moving that I wasn't the only one in the audience with tear-filled eyes. He said that he had been more nervous at that performance than at any since the opening night because his father was in the audience. Then he went on to sing my praises, and said that he owed everything to me.

When the house lights were put on, people started looking around for me. Fortunately we were all standing so I could not be singled out, and Richard sent a posse of stage hands to conduct me and my party backstage. He and Susan had met my friends during the visit to Key West, so there was no need for introductions. We were invited to take tea with them. Richard kept his make-up on for the evening performance to prevent Susan's having to do it twice in the same day.

I had assumed we would be going to a suite in a hotel, the usual accommodation for a star on tour, but to my surprise we were taken to a beautiful house in a very select part of Miami, Golden Beach. It had been rented for a month. Staying with them were Vivienne, Susan's sister, and Vanessa, Vivienne's little girl.

After our enjoyable tea party Richard beckoned me and led the way upstairs. He took me to a lovely front bedroom overlooking a private beach, and he said, 'This is your room.' I told him I couldn't stay and began to explain why. He broke in with, 'Why do you think I took this house?' I was deeply touched and agreed that I would come up for a week in early November and be there for his fifty-fifth birthday on the 10th. Valerie Douglas would also be coming from California.

It was a very happy group that drove back to Key West that night. Our high expectations had been richly fulfilled, and I was eagerly looking forward to my return to Golden Beach, in spite of its being a breach of my no-travel rule. At my insistence, my second visit was made by bus; Richard had wanted to send a car to Key West for me. I was met at the Miami bus terminal and driven to the theatre for the Wednesday matinée. I saw the performance and, rather to my surprise, was again much moved. After the show we went home for a very happy few hours before Richard and Susan returned to the theatre. I didn't go with them but, instead, went to bed at my usual early hour.

After a two-performance day Richard normally stayed in bed until noon, but not this time; he was up at nine. Apart from the excellent meals which she provided for us, Susan left us alone and we talked almost all day, not about *King Lear* or *Richard III*, or about future plans, but about intimate personal matters. The man revealed to me in such talks was very different from the one known to his theatre friends, whom he entertained with tales from his past which became embellished with the years. He needed to talk to me about his hidden self. The boy I had grown to know, admire and love was still there. He didn't try to mitigate or justify the hurt he had caused others, but faced it with deep regret. He remembered gratefully the happy times, and shared his dreams with me; to the end of his life he was a frustrated scholar and writer. One thing I had long esteemed him for was his instinctive generosity. He had made millions, only to give them away. His divorced wives were lavishly provided for. His several brothers and sisters and their children were always treated generously. He had established trusts for his own children. The urge to make money to give him the power to help so many had resulted in his doing much film work he despised, and this, in turn, had resulted in his drinking to drown the sense of artistic guilt.

Before Richard got up the next day – he had caught a heavy

cold and was trying to sweat it out – I did something I had never done before: I walked a couple of miles pushing a pram with a child in it, little Vanessa. As I walked initial embarrassment soon gave way to complete enjoyment.

My talks with Richard on that Friday were very different from those of the day before; they dealt chiefly with Shakespeare, particularly *King Lear*. He had had difficulty with some of his past directors because he had come to the first rehearsal with a clear conception of his part. My idea was that he should be his own director when he played Shakespeare. During the first two weeks of rehearsal his understudy should play his part, while an assistant director sat by Richard and made careful notes of all he said. Then, when Richard took over his part, the assistant director would be in charge. That afternoon Richard and Susan became my audience while I gave them some parts of my lecture-recital on *King Lear*.

There was a matinée on the following Sunday but no evening performance. I went to the matinée and watched most of it from the wings. That viewpoint gives one a special opportunity to judge the integrity of a performance, especially in a musical, when an orchestra separates the audience from the stage; you can see details in an actor's behaviour too small to be noticed by the audience.

That evening, with Susan's ready approval – perhaps it was at her suggestion – Richard and I ate out together at an excellent Chinese restaurant. We had a very happy time exchanging reminiscences. His memory for things long past was remarkable, in sharp contrast to mine. But I noticed that some of the incidents, almost all of them amusing, had received decorative accretions with repeated telling; he was a superb raconteur.

When we got home I gave him a copy of my addresses on the Lord's Prayer to read. I had long felt guilty about not talking to him on religious and spiritual matters. Originally I had not done so because I had not wanted to interfere in his faithful chapel-going with Cis and her family. My own brand of church-going, known in the USA as High Episcopal, was very different. Now I thought and hoped that his reading of my Lenten addresses might begin to bridge the silent gulf. The next morning he gave me back the addresses with some conventional words of praise but made it clear that he didn't want to discuss the subject. I was grieved but tried not to show it.

The next day, Monday 10 November, was Richard's fifty-fifth birthday. When I got up I discovered that Valerie had arrived late the night before, and with her she had brought a whole trunkful of birthday presents. It was very good to see her again. Also, Bob Wilson had arrived. Bob had been Richard's loyal dresser and aide-de-camp for years. Now he was seventy-five and had just emerged from hospital, where he had had a bad time, but he looked remarkably well.

The never-to-be-forgotten wonder of the day was the after-theatre party which Susan had arranged. The whole company had been invited; there were at least a hundred people present. Susan had engaged the premises and services of a really distinguished Miami restaurant. We had the exclusive use of four rooms: a dining room, a dance floor, a bar, and a buffet, which had a most tempting display of delicacies so that guests could continue eating, after the served dinner, through the early hours of the morning. Our family group didn't get home until 2 a.m. and we seemed to be the first to leave.

Richard and I sat at a table for four; the other two places were for Susan and Valerie, but they had so much to see to that they sat down for only an occasional mouthful. Prior to the actual dinner I had enjoyed talking to some members of the company in the bar; some of them seized the opportunity to ask me how they could improve their performance. This had happened with other companies. Richard had always painted such an advance picture of me as the Wonder Man of the Theatre that meeting me must have been a sad disillusionment for many.

When we had come to the end-of-the-meal coffee and liqueur, an imposing gentleman, who may have been the proprietor of the restaurant, came to our table and invited Richard to go with him to the cellar to see their famous wine collection. Richard was away a long time and gradually I became more and more concerned about him; events proved that I was right to be.

Susan came to say that we were going home. She didn't have to tell me the reason; Richard was drunk. He had always taken pains to avoid my seeing him in that state, and apparently he had been commendably sober for months. During the ride home I couldn't make contact with him, and gave up trying. He talked nonstop in an effort, I suppose, to appear normal.

When I saw him the following morning he seemed astonishingly normal, and we had a good talk, with no reference to the wine cellar. Then he said he was going to get an orange juice, and he didn't return. He had lain down on his bed and fallen fast asleep. I was leaving that afternoon, and Susan and I decided we shouldn't wake him because he had a performance in the evening.

It was fortunate that I had again insisted on travelling by bus, because no car could have got through that afternoon. Key West was flooded; it had received a record rainfall of twenty-three inches in twenty-four hours. The roads were littered with stranded cars, their wheels lost to sight in the water. The bus driver went to great trouble to take passengers as near as possible to their homes. Later I wrote to the Greyhound company to commend him for this, and I was glad to hear they had honoured him for it; he came to thank me.

I was the last passenger on board; my house is only a block from the bus terminal. Gary was there to meet me, but he had had to walk. We waded through knee-deep water. When I got home I found, not surprisingly, that the electricity was off. As I think back on it, it seems an appropriate homecoming, because I never saw Richard in person again.

CHAPTER
Sixteen

Fortunately my house had not suffered from the flooding. It is on Solares Hill, which is only sixteen feet above sea level but nonetheless a protection against flooding and against the dreaded destruction by sea surge during a hurricane.

The first morning back home I began to record, to the best of my recollection, the lecture-recital on *King Lear*. I finished it the next day and sent it to Richard, who called me a few days later to talk about it. I was increasingly concerned about the state of his health, and so was grateful to be kept busy in the early months of 1981. I had agreed to give ten public lectures on Shakespeare, one a week, at the Tennessee Williams Fine Arts Center.

On Wednesday 11 March I was surprised to receive a call from Chen Sam, a delightful lady who could, I suppose, be described as Elizabeth's press representative, but is much more than that. It was virtually a command, which I was excitedly happy to obey, to go to Fort Lauderdale the following Saturday to see Elizabeth in *The Little Foxes*. She had remembered that I would not stay overnight, so I was to see the matinée. I would be met at Miami airport by THE car, a Rolls-Royce, which had already received much photographic publicity.

I took the 10 a.m. flight on the Saturday and was indeed met by the eye-popping wonder, which was driven by a very pleasant chauffeur, Frank Grady. True to form, Elizabeth was not waiting to welcome me; clocks never governed her life. She had been up the previous night until 4 a.m. and was still asleep.

She had two performances ahead of her that day and so must be allowed to sleep until the last possible moment. She was staying at Turnberry Isle which, from what I saw that afternoon, was a lavish vacation home for the overfed and underdressed. While we waited for Elizabeth to wake up, Frank Grady and I enjoyed lunch together.

The reunion with Elizabeth was delightful but, as usual, she was late, and very soon we set off together in the limousine. She was so late that she had to do her make-up in the car, which was solidly built and never once jolted us. As we hurried along we shared thoughts and recollections. She was annoyed because a local journalist who had interviewed her had omitted her reference to my part in her first stage appearance, the poetry reading for AMDA, seventeen years before. Of course we talked about Richard; she showed genuine concern at his deteriorating physical condition, about which she seemed to be well informed.

As for *The Little Foxes*, I had reservations about the production but none about Elizabeth. The impact of her stage presence was remarkable, and her keen intelligence was very obvious in her portrayal of Regina. After the performance we had a brief chat in her dressing room and then I left to catch the 6 p.m. flight home.

A week later Richard had to leave the cast of *Camelot* permanently. He went into hospital for a cervical operation which had to be postponed twice because of his poor general condition. Characteristically he was not co-operating with the doctors, who sent him home temporarily in order to improve his capacity to undergo the operation. I could readily imagine what a bad time Susan was having, but she was successful in changing his attitude to his doctors, and he returned to the hospital in a fit state, physically and mentally, for the operation.

It was performed on 22 April. On the same day I went to Miami for what seemed to be shaping into an annual lecture-recital; this time the subject was *Macbeth*. I calculated that he was on the operating table at the same time that I was on the stage. My ordeal was successful and I was deeply relieved to hear later that Richard's had also been. But he would be out of action for six months. How would he stand that? And how would Susan manage to cope with him? A week later Valerie gave me a not unexpected report: the patient was physically better but temperamentally very difficult. He had never been able to endure physical frustration. On the eleventh day after the operation he left the hospital, and that release improved his attitude.

A few weeks of silence followed, but I was used to those. For my own peace of mind I tried to assume this meant that Richard was making satisfactory progress. Finally, in early June, I wrote to him; I had to wait another three weeks for a reply. His news was apparently good but one thing worried me: he and Susan were flying home to Switzerland, and he was getting away from the care of the California doctors. They had prescribed a very strict regimen for him, but would he adhere to it?

A month later I saw him on television. The occasion was the royal wedding of Prince Charles to Lady Diana. Richard looked gaunt. He was certainly not observing the desirable six months of inactivity. Three weeks later Valerie flew to Celigny; Susan needed her help.

On 8 August I had a long call from Richard, the first of several during the next few weeks, some of them lasting as long as ninety minutes. He wanted my co-operation in an ambitious new scheme. I felt it had been prompted by his enforced lack of activity, and had probably been suggested by a London businessman involved in show business, who was to be his partner. It immediately involved me in morning-to-night work for three weeks; if it had matured, it would have kept me busy for the rest of my life. I was to supply Richard with lists of plays, chiefly revivals, suitable for production first in London and then in New York, to be followed by films derived from the productions. I was to give brief synopses of the plays with some comments on them and their staging. I originally assumed that the plays were to be vehicles for Richard, and my first list of suggestions had this in mind, but in one of our long phone conversations he was joined by his London partner who made it quite clear that this was a major business venture involving much more than Richard as an actor. My instinctive response to that was negative – I had no desire to see Richard become just a producer – but I extended the range of my work with his encouragement; he had been very happy with my first list of suggestions. Altogether I sent five long lists, the last typically containing twenty-two plays. For some I had suggested Elizabeth as the star. But after all my work, the whole thing came to nothing, in fact and in payment. I was relieved for Richard but a bit sorry for myself.

On 16 September I heard from Valerie, not Richard, that he was in Los Angeles again. He had been persuaded to return to the care of the California doctors; he must have felt bad to agree to that. The doctors had said that in terms of his post-operative condition he was back to square one. Then on 2 October both Susan and Valerie called me; during the night Richard had had an operation for a perforated ulcer. I felt it was yet another example of how the mind can affect the body. A week later Valerie called to tell me that he was still in hospital but expected to be out in a few days. As before, incarceration in a hospital was having a bad effect on his mental state. The rumour was abroad that he had terminal cancer. Why do people enjoy believing the worst about others?

Later in the month I was relieved to hear that Richard was sufficiently recovered to be planning the next move, and a major one, in his professional career. He had agreed to play Wagner in a film about the composer. It was to turn out to be indeed a major production, with a cast including Laurence Olivier, John Gielgud, Ralph Richardson and Vanessa Redgrave; it was to be filmed on location in Germany. The result would be a film that lasts for nine hours. I have heard wonderful reports of it and read similarly enthusiastic reviews but, as I write this, no arrangements have yet been concluded for the public showing of it in the USA, either in cinemas or on television.

When I next saw Richard, early in the new year, he was doing an interview on television and, to my great relief, he looked better than I feared he would. But another fear of mine was only too amply fulfilled: he and Susan were getting a divorce. The strain upon the wife of the difficult invalid had been too much. And I was very depressed by some news from Valerie: Richard in London had taken to the bottle with his old zest. I suppose it was in reaction to his fourth divorce, counting the two from Elizabeth. In a reading of *Under Milk Wood*, the night before the memorial service for Dylan Thomas in Westminster Abbey, he had been incoherent.

Then it was my turn to go into hospital. For many years I had had some gall-bladder trouble, but the condition of my heart had made an operation inadvisable. During a night in June the pain became so bad that it was decided the gall-bladder had to be removed. After a week of medication I was operated on with complete success. It gave me a momentary sense of absurd pride when I learned later that some of the gallstones were the biggest the doctors had ever seen, and I understood that they were to be sent to a medical museum! Christian was in Martha's Vineyard when I was taken ill, but as soon as he heard about the imminent operation he flew down, and his caring presence did much to ensure my speedy recovery.

Among the many flowers I received during my convalescence were some from Richard and some from Valerie. As soon as I was well enough, Valerie called me to report on Richard, who was making the Wagner film in Europe. He had a new girlfriend, Sally Hay, whom he had met while she was working on the production side of the film. She was to become his last wife and a dear friend of mine. Sally helped him with his drink problem, which was causing trouble on the set. Also at this time both Richard and I were delighted to hear that Kate had scored a success on Broadway in a revival of Noël Coward's *Present Laughter*, in which the star was George C. Scott.

I was surprised when, having finished work on the Wagner film, Richard returned to California for further treatment, accompanied by Sally. A week later I had a call from Richard which made me very happy; he assured me that all was well with him, and I believed him, all the more when I saw him in a television interview a few months later looking better than he had for years.

The BBC was planning to do a television programme on Richard, and he was angry that I had been approached about it when I was recovering from an operation. But ultimately, in December, I did contribute to it. The BBC sent a crew of five to film an interview with me. It took place in my study and was a very happy experience. The interviewer was a charming new acquaintance, James Fenton, a poet much acclaimed by the cognoscenti. He had been described as 'the most talented poet of his generation', but I confess that I had been unaware of him; Key West is 5,000 miles from London in more ways than are shown on the map. He left with me a copy of his recently published book of poems *The Memory of War*. I often read a poem in it and remember James Fenton with admiration.

The year I've been dealing with was 1982, and I was very busy at both ends of it. In January a professor who was an acquaintance of mine had asked to read my work on Burgoyne. He seemed genuinely enthusiastic about it and suggested that I should record it, especially since it was written in the first person. That was the beginning of a long process which resulted in the public-broadcasting radio station in Amherst, Massachusetts, putting out twenty-six half-hour readings from *They Called Me Gentleman Johnny*. I should have been willing to do the recordings for nothing just to give my writing a hearing, but it seemed I had to have a professional fee and to resume temporarily my membership of AFTRA (the American Federation of Television and Radio Artists). But where was the money coming from? Here some friends of mine from St Louis, Missouri, stepped in. They were David and Susan Mesker, and they had a trust fund which made disbursements for just such projects. I had got to know them because they have a winter home in Key West. Susan spends much more time in it than David is able to, and she had attended my local lectures assiduously. The recordings of my readings were made at a radio station in Key West, but all expenses, in addition to my fee, were covered by the Mesker grant. The readings were broadcast from forty-four PBS stations throughout the country, but alas, not from one we could get in Key West. I had some appreciative letters from listeners, most of them from California. All wanted to know where they could get a copy of the book!

Late in the same year Emlyn Williams arrived in Key West. I was very happy that he had included the island on a tour of his remarkable Dickens recitals. He performed in the same theatre where I had given my Shakespeare lectures. I longed to spend hours with him but he was here at the same time as the BBC television team. I had invited two of them, who were from Wales, to lunch, and Emlyn joined us. It was all very enjoyable but I ached for a private talk with Emlyn, and he did manage to stay for almost an hour after the others had left. Of course our subject was Richard, and he urged me to write the story of our relationship. Thus the seed was planted that has resulted in this book, but in my Christmas letter to him in London I said quite definitely that I could not write such a book, and gave him the reasons. Three years later I changed my mind and I wrote to him at once about it. I sent my letter to London, not knowing that he was on another transatlantic tour. He was in Toronto, but my letter was read to him over the phone. He wanted to reply to me there and then, but had been given reason to doubt the reliability of the Canadian postal service, so he waited until he got to Los Angeles. There he mailed it on 21 January 1986. It was perfectly addressed but I did not receive it until 25 April! So much for the United States postal service. When I complained, all I got was, 'Things like that happen.' Emlyn wrote, 'Needless to say I am thrilled you are changing your mind and will put pen to paper, and I'd like to think I've helped a little to change it!' He had, and I am very grateful to him.

In many ways my life in the following year, 1983, seemed to epitomize retirement at its best: I thoroughly enjoyed good health, wonderful friends and long-delayed reading, but professionally I did nothing. I knew it couldn't last; it was too much like giving up and waiting for the end. I resumed full activity in 1984 – until the end came for Richard.

But while I was taking things easy, Richard was as busy as ever. Early in the year I had a call from Valerie to say that he wanted to come to see me and hoped to do so soon, but then a canny producer persuaded him to star with Elizabeth in a production of Noël Coward's *Private Lives*. (A friend of mine suggested it should be renamed *Public Lives*.) I was urged by Elizabeth to go to the opening night on Broadway, but Richard knew that I wouldn't travel; more than once he had mentioned his disappointment at my not seeing him in *Equus*. My contribution to the first night on 7 May was some photographs for the special programme, and telegrams of good wishes to both Richard and Elizabeth.

They had agreed to do the show for six months, including a tour of several cities. I gathered it was not a happy experience for either of them. Richard was frequently irritated by Elizabeth's failure to adapt to the discipline of theatre, as in the matter of punctuality, and Elizabeth must have been irritated with equal frequency by the constant presence of Sally, which reached its climax on Sunday 3 July in Los Angeles when Sally became the fourth Mrs Richard Burton. On the Monday a very happy Richard called to tell me about it. The following day I sent flowers to Sally and spoke to both the newlyweds.

A week before the wedding I had seen, through the kindness of a friend, a Cinemax copy of the Jules Dassin film *Circle of Two*, which Richard had made in Canada. It was very much better than I feared it would be, and I could not and cannot understand why it did not receive general distribution; it was infinitely better than some of Richard's films that did.

I was very surprised to get two long calls from Richard on the same day in August. Not for the first time the calls had been prompted by a need for help. He had been approached to do a television series of poetry readings. What should be the shape of it? Chronological? Subject matter? Each programme devoted to one poet? Or one verse form? It was finally decided that I should make a recording of my lecture *The Magic of Poetry* and sent it to him in Washington, DC together with a long letter. I had both in the mail by three o'clock the following day.

Private Lives closed on 6 November and Richard and Sally lost no time in going to Haiti, where they bought a four-storey house. In spite of the trouble involved in turning a house into a home, they didn't forget my seventy-ninth birthday; I had a long and happy conversation with both of them. All three of us eagerly and confidently looked forward to their coming to Key West on their way back to Europe, but before that they wanted me to join them in Haiti for Christmas. My no-travel rule forbade that. I had broken it for Golden Beach; why not for Haiti? This time my NO was adamant, and Richard accepted it. Then we went on to talk about Dylan Thomas; he was very interested to hear that I had done a transatlantic interview by telephone with the BBC in Wales on the subject of Dylan. It brought back memories of a Sunday morning forty years before when he had introduced me to Dylan's work by discovering a poem in an old newspaper. I have much regretted that I didn't break my rule a second time and go to Haiti, because Richard and Sally were unable to make their promised visit to Key West; a film engagement – it must have been *Nineteen Eighty-Four* – took them back to Europe sooner than they expected.

In the early months of 1984 I amply made up for my pleasant idleness of the year before, giving solo readings and more Lenten addresses in St Paul's Church, adjudicating – along with José Ferrer – in a high-school Shakespeare competition, and delivering my own lecture-recital *A Portrait of Hamlet*. I was worried that I wouldn't be at my best for this last performance, but I needn't have been. I find the most difficult aspect of my ageing is loss of memory, particularly of people; scarcely a day passes without some embarrassment resulting from it. The strange anomaly is that my memory for lines, especially Shakespeare's, remains good.

Soon after this I was honoured to be asked, apparently at the request of the students, to give the commencement address for the graduating students at the excellent Florida Keys Community College. It was gratifying to see many mature students among the graduates, and even some senior citizens. I welcomed the opportunity to express my deep appreciation of the great blessings that ten years' full-time residence in Key West had bestowed upon me.

It was not until May that I received two long calls on the same day from Richard, who was at home in Celigny. The ostensible reason for the first call was that he wanted me to send him a copy of my book *The Sole Voice* for A.L. Rowse. I was to send it to London, where he was going very soon, and where he expected to meet Rowse. Richard was obviously in an unusually good mood. He said he felt better than he had for years, and it was all due to Sally. He longed for me to meet her, and he was definitely going to bring her to Key West in late January or early February of 1985. What's more, they would stay for several weeks so that we could study *King Lear* together, and also my new version of *Richard III*. He was excited about his part in the film of George Orwell's *Nineteen Eighty-Four*, and planned to bring some humanity to the apparently inhuman O'Brien. Then he talked about *Ellis Island*, a television series based on a novel; he had agreed to do it because Kate would be in it, and he would have some scenes with her. After that came a film to be made largely in Germany, and at the end of the year he would go to India to make *The Quiet American*, from the novel by Graham Greene . . . and then Key West. It was years since I had heard such a happy Richard.

The second call was prompted by something he had forgotten in the first call. It was to ask me to write to Cis; she was feeling her age and would welcome a letter from me. He would be seeing her soon at her home, which was near London. Mention of Cis unleashed many memories. Richard was not a man who wore his heart on his sleeve, but in that conversation he revived deep memories that we shared and treasured. It was a revelation of his true values, and as such warmly remembered by me.

He called me again after he had finished both *Nineteen Eighty-Four* and *Ellis Island*. He was very happy about the former but wanted to emphasize that the only reason he was in the television series was to be with Kate. Both to him and, when I had seen it, to me, *Ellis Island* was a shameful exploitation of a great subject. However, he had had a fine time with Kate, both on and off the set. It had long seemed to me that he felt a sense of guilt at his neglect of Kate, so that working together must have been a very rewarding experience for both of them. Again he went on about how well he felt and how happy he was with Sally. This was in mid-July.

And then, on 6 August, at 9.20 in the morning, Valerie called to tell me that Richard was dead. Sybil also called to give me the news. It was the greatest shock I had ever experienced because it was so completely without warning; on the contrary, he himself had led me to believe that his physical ailments were definitely disappearing – more than once he had told me recently that he felt better than he had for years. Later I heard from Sally that he had complained of a pain in the head, and then he seemed to fall asleep, but he never woke up. He was taken to a local hospital and then to one in Geneva, all to no avail. As I gradually accepted the fact that he was gone, I realized that it had been a merciful death for him, but for those who loved him it could hardly have been more devastating.

There followed a horrendous few days which left me utterly exhausted. I was besieged by interviewers. My telephone number has long been unlisted, but I received calls from as far away as California and Germany. I don't know how they obtained my number; I'm certain that the telephone company did not reveal it. On two occasions the callers had persuaded the police to intercede for them, and officers came to my door. One man who worked for a magazine in Germany found his own way there, complete with camera.

Richard was buried in Celigny. He had made his wishes in this matter very clear by purchasing a plot to receive his body. It was a great disappointment to his Welsh family, who had wanted him to be buried in his birthplace, but they were well represented at the funeral. I was not there, nor at the memorials to him in New York and London. After the one in London I had a most welcome and consoling call from Elizabeth and Kate, who were together. Richard would have appreciated that; Elizabeth had always felt guilty about breaking up his first marriage, and now his death had brought her together with the child of that marriage.

After the ordeal of the interviews was over, the calls and letters of sympathy continued for a few weeks, but those were welcome, some of them very much so, especially ones which revived happy memories of Richard. I answered nearly 150 of them by hand, but this was not a chore because my thoughts were filled with Richard, and it was somehow a comfort to write about him. Another comfort at this time was meeting Sally sooner than I had expected. She came to Key West just fifteen days after his death. Valerie had called me from Europe to say that they were coming; they had to go to Haiti in connection with the estate, and then California, and they would visit me en route, just for a day.

They arrived late at night. They had thought it would be necessary to spend the night in Miami, but they caught the last flight to Key West. Valerie telephoned but, as she expected, I was already in bed. They insisted on not disturbing me, and went to a hotel. In the morning, at my request, Gary picked them up and, after they had had lunch with me, he came to take them to the airport. There was an immediate rapport between Sally and me; we each knew and were grateful for what the other had done for Richard and meant to him. She is beautiful, sensitive and intelligent but, as I reflect on it, so in their different ways were the other three wives. But they had made new lives for themselves without Richard; she was his widow.

As for Valerie she had worked for and with him for some thirty years. She had known him at his best and worst. More than once she had been tempted to leave him, but fortunately she had stayed. Even in death he had left her with a heavy burden, having made her the executrix of his will, which prevented her from undertaking any other work until it was settled. Moreover, it proved to present a great problem: Richard had been a legal resident of Switzerland for almost twenty years and the will had been drawn up in Geneva, but it was to be executed in London, and so the tiresome and expensive law's delay became inevitable. Valerie and I remain good friends.

Once she had met me, Sally kept in frequent touch by letter and telephone. She, as Richard was and I am, is a bibliophile, and Richard's last little gift to her was a book, Barbara Pym's *A Very Private Eye*; Sally gave it to me. Richard knew that Sally liked the novels of Barbara Pym. The book consists of posthumous selections from her diaries, and it reveals a woman that Sally would admire because they share some excellent qualities: intelligence, wit, sensitivity, independence. In proof of that last-named attribute Sally has already embarked on a career as a writer, at this stage primarily as a journalist, but I feel sure she will advance from the factual to the creative.

Among the many tributes and memorials to Richard, one was totally unexpected and I was deeply moved by it. A former student at AMDA, Ronald Souza, who had given up the theatre to become a successful farmer in California, had been a great admirer of Richard. He sent me a cheque for $2,500. After consulting with him, it was decided that the money should be given as a memorial to Richard as follows: $1,500 to be divided between two charities of which he would have approved, and $1,000 towards the purchase of some festival vestments for St Paul's Church; I would make up the balance of the cost. Richard's name is on the vestments, which are very beautiful. They are used only at high festivals like Christmas and Easter, when the sight of them brings Richard to mind, not only for me but for many of the congregation. They had seen him with me at St Paul's, the only church, to the best of my recollection, where we had attended a service together.

Less than four months after Richard's death I celebrated my eightieth birthday, and my friends saw to it that it truly was a celebration, from morning to night. Gary gave a memorable dinner party for me in a private room of an excellent restaurant. In addition to very close local friends, others came from New York and New Jersey, and one from Europe – Sally. She stayed with me for five precious days. If Richard had been alive, his film commitments would probably have prevented her from coming. Valerie was unable to attend but a gift of beautiful flowers represented her at the party.

As we all ate, drank and laughed together, I had a vivid memory which I did not share with the company. During one of our private sessions when Richard and Susan stayed with me in Key West, he had said how much he regretted that he was born twenty days too soon to be legally my son, but in spite of the law he was exactly that. Then he said, 'Just think of it: when you are eighty, I won't even be sixty.' He wasn't even fifty-nine.

'He didn't adopt me; I adopted him.' What would have happened to him if he hadn't become my son, in all but the law? The most striking thing about Richard was the impact of his personality; he didn't have to do or say anything. This is what gave him such a powerful stage presence. He was big, in his gifts and in his faults, in his affections and in his dislikes. As I have said, there were many times when he despised acting as kids' games, especially when he was making a rubbishy film; on the other hand he was completely fulfilled in his great moments on the stage. He was an inveterate reader of great literature – and I think he would have become that without me – and so inevitably he dreamed of becoming a good writer, but I doubt that the essentially hermitic life of a full-time writer would have satisfied him. He needed public contact. Perhaps academia would have made him happy, especially if he had been at Oxford University. Then again, as I first thought, he might have fulfilled himself in politics, but he reacted strongly to tales of political corruption at a local level in South Wales; he remained cynically disillusioned about this element in political life. Yet he never lost his deep feeling for the interests of the working class, and I suppose it gave him a kind of inner guilt when he made millions and remembered the poverty and hardships of the Welsh coalfields in the bad days. This was what caused him to be so generous in his gifts to his Welsh family. And it was a sense of guilt, too, that made him generous in his divorce settlements.

In spite of his faults, none of them petty, I remember Richard with pride in his best achievements and with gratitude for a fulfilling paternal relationship that lasted over forty years, and still remains deep within me.